FROM OVER THE EDGE

A Christian's guide to surviving Breakdown & Depression

— JON GROGAN —

Sacristy
Press

Sacristy Press
PO Box 612, Durham, DH1 9HT

www.sacristy.co.uk

First published in 2016 by Sacristy Press, Durham

Sacristy Limited, registered in England & Wales, number 7565667

British Library Cataloguing-in-Publication Data
A catalogue record for the book is available from the British Library

ISBN 978–1–910519–22–6

To the quiet, brave ones.

PREFACE

I suppose it would be a good idea for me to say something right at the beginning about what this book is about and who it is aimed at.

Or it might be easier to first say what the book *isn't*. Although I ended up incorporating much more of my own personal experience in the book than I expected I would, I didn't really set out to write a memoir of my experience of suffering from depressive illness, and I still don't think this book belongs to that genre. There are books out there written by people who are much more talented and eloquent at describing what for me has so often felt like the indescribable.[1] After all, I am a lawyer, and the sort of writing that I am more familiar with involves persuading people about the merits of particular arguments, normally supported by evidence which has been sifted through and analysed carefully. I have always liked the way Norman Anderson, whilst not intending to be "presumptuous or provocative", still felt able to carve out a role as "A Lawyer Among the Theologians" in his book of that name.[2] Whilst conscious of the need of an even greater degree of modesty should

I be considered for the role, I wonder if perhaps there might also be space for a lawyer among the psychologists and psychiatrists? I certainly expect that my analytical training has rubbed off in the way I have approached the subject of this book. But whilst I have come to feel quite strongly about certain issues covered, I never intended it to turn into a polemic, so forgive me if I ever start to sound like I'm getting up on my soapbox.

No, first and foremost this is a book written by a sufferer, aimed at fellow sufferers, to help them get better. To help them get back up from over the edge.

But could there be others who might benefit from reading? I appreciate that there may be some people picking the book up who have not fallen over the edge, but will feel as though they are teetering. I do hope there are things in here that might help them work out what preventative measures they could put in place before a full-blown breakdown ensues. Indeed, I suspect there are aspects of the wisdom from over the edge that will speak to many people who are feeling challenged by and dissatisfied with aspects of our highly-pressurised, busy, noisy modern day society.

I also wanted this to be a book that could be used by loved ones trying to understand what the sufferer is going through. After all, depressive illness doesn't affect just the individual patient; its ripples spread far and wide. With this in mind I have tried to write a relatively practical book. I say *relatively*, because I have found that some of the ideas and concepts discussed in the book are not immediately graspable. If only it were as easy as thumbing up a depression instruction manual to tell us what to do next (or maybe not—I mean, might that be missing the point?). But I still wanted to write something which my family and friends might have found useful when the illness suddenly took a grip and the seriousness of the situation became all too frighteningly apparent. There were some dark times, the memory of which can still cause me to shudder, which we spent floundering and panicking in utter confusion and terror, trying to make important decisions about what type of support we needed to access, whether medical, psychological, or spiritual.

The truth is that although so much remains a mystery about this illness, there is an incredible amount of understanding and insight to be gained as a sufferer. One psychiatrist friend once referred to depression as being "very treatable". Now maybe my friend was only thinking in relative terms, comparing the treatability of depression with more challenging forms of mental illness. But as we will see, people's experience of receiving medical treatment for clinical depression can prove to be rather less straightforward than this view would suggest. I also know that psychological or spiritual advice which has the ability to really address the heart of things can be elusive—even when we do come across it, we may not stick with it, not trusting its counter-intuitive nature. But it does come as such a relief when we begin to appreciate that there is a great deal that can be done to help us get well again. And if more of us sufferers can share our experience of what we have learned, what we are glad to have persevered with, I'm sure we will help rob depression of some of its destructive power. I see this book as part of my contribution to that discussion.

As a Christian, the spiritual dimension to what I have gone through has been of huge importance to me. As we will see, on occasion, this has involved having to test whether certain views I came across were indeed authentic Christian ones. It is amazing how our experience of suffering can often take on the role of a sort of relentless truth probe. But whilst we might struggle intensely to relate our Christian faith to mental suffering, it is my firm belief that it will only be through our openness to God that we will finally find all truth and wholeness, and how the longed-for cure of our illness will ultimately be transformed into real and lasting healing. First and foremost, I hope that any sufferer reading this book might feel encouraged, understood, and, hopefully, a little bit better. But I would also hope that they might be helped to discover new dimensions to their faith through this awful experience—dimensions which will not only sustain them during their illness, but also in their life beyond.

Finally, I need to say something about the type of depressive illness that I have suffered from and which I am primarily discussing in the book. The word "depression" itself can be a real obstacle when it comes to definitions and labels, with most people (well, most non-medical people) only associating the word with how we feel when it rains a lot. This can be why well-meaning loved ones often search in desperation for ways to "cheer up" the sufferer in their midst. How painful it is to everyone concerned when such kindly acts only serve to make matters worse. The sufferer might feel that telling friends and family that they have "depression" or even "clinical depression" simply does not cut it—it seems our current lexicon is found wanting when it comes to identifying something which people can recognise as a debilitating illness involving serious chemical imbalances in the brain. Robert Burton's description of the illness in his seventeenth century classic, *The Anatomy of Melancholy*, certainly comes close to describing the awfulness of the condition:

> If there be a hell upon earth, it is to be found in a melancholy man's heart . . . I say of our melancholy man, he is the cream of human adversity, the quintessence, and upshot; all other diseases whatsoever, are but flea-bitings to melancholy in extent: 'Tis the pith of them all[.][3]

With hindsight, I can also now see that when I have talked to some people who have experienced depression, or have read certain authors' books about depression, we have actually been at cross-purposes because of the failure to recognise significant differences in our respective conditions. I'm not sure whether the person who coined the phrase "depression is the common cold of mental health problems" ever suffered depression him or herself. I tend to view having a cold as a minor inconvenience—something which my immune system should be able to cope with fairly easily. But whilst some sufferers may be able to relate to that description of their illness, others might feel as though they have contracted the mental health equivalent of double pneumonia. And, just like a pneumonia patient, they may have to be hospitalised so that they can receive the intensive type of care needed to get better.

In previous years, my own version of the illness would have probably been described as a form of mental or nervous breakdown. I am not sure whether those terms were ever medically recognised, but in any event, nowadays I would be more likely to be diagnosed as having suffered a depressive episode (which sounds far less dramatic). Depressive episodes are typically diagnosed as being mild, moderate or severe, although other classifications may be found.[4]

Some people reading this book may share some of the symptoms I have experienced, but not others, and some might have symptoms of their own that I would not readily recognise. Whilst I think it is useful that we bear in mind that there may be differences between our "depressions", I hope that you will find this book useful, whatever the severity or type of depression you are suffering from.

So, with those preliminaries over, I was about to say I hope you enjoy the book, but I know that probably isn't the right sentiment. I know, even now, that on certain days I can't bring myself to read or watch stuff about depression. I have to be in the right mood. This tends to mean that my proximity to the illness and its symptoms is such that various questions are still being raised in my mind, answers to which will require further insight (let's face it, who reads books about depression for fun?). But I also know that it can be tough when at a low ebb to be taken out of your comfort zone by having pre-conceived views about quite personal things challenged. I've tried to bear that in mind, and hope that even those feeling at their most fragile might be able to dip in and out of the book and find something helpful and positive.

ACKNOWLEDGEMENTS

This endeavour has only been made possible because of such a brilliant support network of friends, family and beyond. Obvious thanks to Fiona and the girls for bearing with me when such a short book seemed to be taking forever. Special thanks to my Dad, Reg, for checking out some early and very draft chapters and assuring me that people, including himself, might want to read such a book. Also to my friend Jenny, who undertook a more thorough and most thought-provoking review. An important credit too to Dr Rachel Cullinan for having carried out a medical review of the content of the book.

And thanks to the same network of people for remaining with me during my time "over the edge", for sticking with me when, quite frankly, none of us knew what to do.

Let's hope this book helps people in a similar predicament.

CONTENTS

1. WHY BOTHER?

Blessed be the God and Father of our Lord Jesus Christ,
the Father of mercies and God of all comfort, who
comforts us in all our afflictions, so that we may be
able to comfort those who are in any affliction, with the
comfort with which we ourselves are comforted by God.
2 Corinthians 1:3–4 (ESV)

Do you remember when you were a kid (I still do this actually) and you sang along to pop tunes, oblivious to the intended meaning of the song? You simply used your own mangled lyrics, your own naive interpretation of what was being sung. Recently, my daughter came up with a fantastic example of the art form when she started singing John Denver's "Annie's Song" with new lyrics: "You build up my fences . . ". I also particularly enjoyed once hearing someone blast out the chorus of one of Mr Mister's hit songs from the 1980s. "Carry a laser!" was the command the singer kept repeating, somewhat implausibly it has to be said. The correct lyric

and the title of the song is, of course, "Kyrie Eleison".
Christ have mercy.

I love Carole King's "Too Much Rain". In one of the
verses, and I'm paraphrasing here, the singer wants
to discern what makes her tick; she has clearly been
hurt emotionally and wants to protect herself from
any more pain. And how will she be able to apply this
self-knowledge? Well, in my own previously mangled
version, she was going to *"write it down"*. Yes, every
jot of it. Nothing to be left out. I now know that those
aren't quite the right lyrics, but I still like this idea of
our trying to capture on paper what we have come to
fully understand, a documenting process that has both
therapeutic and preventative qualities. And I will always
associate this with Carole King.

So, I told myself that even if no-one was interested in
publishing this book, writing it would still be a useful
thing for me to do. At one level it could prove to be a
resource for me in the future should, heaven forbid,
something similar ever befall me again. It's amazing how
much of the horror story your memory wipes clear, with
only the echoes of certain symptoms being felt months
or years down the line, triggered by some temporary
setback or other. But the exercise seemed more than
this. The thing is, for the best part of three years, I kept
a journal, starting with what I can now look back and
recognise as being a second breakdown (the first one
had happened only a year or so earlier, but the recovery
from it had been far from secure). I have never kept a

journal before, but a kind and wise friend bought a nice hard-backed note book plus pen and commended them to me as being useful tools to help me on the road to recovery. I took to the journal slowly and sporadically at first, but soon found that thoughts, insights, other people's comments and quotations from books were making strong impressions on me, and that, somehow, I had to get things down on paper as part of what felt like a channelling of something that was working within me. With my mind broken and disturbed, the pages of the journal helped lend some kind of stability and objectivity to what has been the most truly terrifying experience of my life. On a fairly deep level, I also felt an assurance that there was a spiritual dimension to the process; that God was involved in this new-found written eloquence, this re-connectedness. Some stuff I wrote was admittedly a bit obscure and hasn't stuck with me. But much of it has, and this material has been the main inspiration for writing this book.

The people of Israel gave God many names to represent different aspects of his character. A preacher in our church once challenged us to think about what names we would want to give to God; what names we could think of to reflect our own experience of God in our different circumstances and stages of life. Suggestions included "God of surprises", "God of humour" and "God of peace", all of which I could relate to. But for me, the name that came most strongly to mind was the "God of connections"; the God of one-thing-leading-to-another, of illuminating the right verse in a song, or something during a conversation with a friend, or a snippet on the radio. The God of the right book being somehow added to my reading list, of bringing insight just when I've needed it. The connections have felt like so much more than mere serendipity, but when I have been tempted to doubt God's special providence during this period of my life, my journal has stood as a form of testimony to what I have learned so far.

Researching and writing this book has also brought a form of closure to this period in my life; a joining-up of the scribblings in my journal, a levelling-off (please God) of the steepest and longest learning curve that I ever thought was imaginable. St Ignatius of Loyola (more of him to come later on) experienced an extremely intense and formative time during a period of being laid low (the cause of his indisposition was a cannonball rather than mental illness). Looking back at that time, he later referred to God as having trained him as a school teacher teaches a schoolboy. I expect St Ignatius would have agreed that the learning process with God never ends, but I think we are right to discern different stages and periods of our life as having different purposes, different emphases. It feels to me that my "journal period" has been a special time when the Lord was training me, not only about how to get through the immediate suffering, but to learn things for whatever might lie ahead.

This has been a highly introspective time of my life. Depression in all its forms probably leads the sufferer to spend more time alone than they would if functioning normally. At times, you simply cannot bear to be in the company of others; the distortion of reality that you are experiencing is just too much to allow any form of social interaction. This enforced form of solitary confinement has been seen as a way of explaining the evolutionary purpose of the illness, with the retreat from daily activities providing the necessary environment for sufferers to re-evaluate their lives and analyse the issues that contributed towards the onset of the condition. It felt to me that some of the things I learned "in solitary" were probably for my consumption only—secret things revealed by God. But much seemed capable of being turned from inwards to outwards. I was challenged by 2 Corinthians 1:3 and was left feeling compelled to "do something" with the comfort that I began to recognise as coming from God. But even when writing almost felt like the fulfilling of a duty, it did not feel like a slavish one, but more the outworking of a desire to tell it as it is for a new generation of sufferers. As Margaret Silf puts it, "when someone dares to pierce the darkness a new source of light is opened up for those who still dwell in the night." She explains that the darkness we pierce is "our own darkness", our own suffering. And the transformation from darkness to a star lighting up the night sky only works if we are prepared to pierce through the night "with trust and courage, without evasion or circumvention".[5] My hope is that the insights that I have gained, and the consolation that I have experienced, can now become "connections" (or constellations?) for others going through a similarly dark time in their lives.

I realise that by sharing my experience with you in this way I am standing on holy ground. For all sufferers that have, or are given, eyes to see and ears to hear, their recovery from depression will be a time when God not only feels incredibly distant but also incredibly close—closer probably than they have ever experienced him before. And so *your* lessons, *your* insights, will be different to mine. Your healing will take a different form to mine. Your way will be God's way for you and you only. All I am asking, as one fellow pilgrim to another, is if I may walk (or climb) with you for a few miles. It's just that I may have some understanding of what you might be going through and what might still lie ahead. You see, I already walked this route a few years ago. I'm now singing a different tune to the one I sang when I started out. The new tune has so much more depth and soul than the old one, and even when it shifts into a minor key—come to think of it, especially when it shifts into a minor key—it touches me and helps sustain me as I continue to journey on. Forgive me if I can't help singing it as we walk. And I'll try not to mangle the lyrics.

2. THE BIG ONE

And we know that in all things God works
for the good of those who love him, who have
been called according to his purpose.
Romans 8:28

OK, so you're over the Edge.

And your body wants you to have no doubt about it. To borrow from C. S. Lewis's metaphor, it is acting as a megaphone, screaming out that it just cannot carry on. It thinks it has no alternative but to stop you in your tracks, quite literally.

And precisely because of the seriousness of your condition, finding the way out of this is likely to take time. Don't be too hopeful about finding short-cuts. We are not in easy-fix territory.

The good news, however, is that, despite breaking down on you in such a spectacular fashion, your body still wants to help you get out of this dilemma. There's no need to fight against yourself, is what I think I'm trying to say. But for the plan to really work, the way out is also going to have to be a way which is going to sustain you, holistically, for the rest of your post-breakdown life, and ultimately help you become the person God wants you to be.

The image of the crucible has often been linked with suffering. I have certainly found it useful in understanding aspects of depressive illness. You find yourself in this unbearable place, where all of the negative emotions and anxieties that you have ever felt in the past suddenly get intensified in the heat of the furnace. You feel them like you've never felt them before. But, gradually, they become exposed as dross, and as they float to the surface you see clearly, maybe for the first time, that they were counterfeits all along. They were never part of the "real you", but instead belonged to the realm of fear, and we know that God calls us, invites us, to a life of joy, the opposite of fear. Joy—a much more substantial and permanent state of being than mere "happiness", note. And, finally, we start to recognise that the pure metal emerging in the refining process is that part of us which is true and lasting and helps connect us to God. It is a form of homecoming, really.

Music has played a large part in the healing process for me. Peter Meadows, in his book *Pressure Points*, recalls his wife Rosemary filling the house with the sound of Barbara Streisand's "Never Give Up" when she was suffering from depression.[6] Maybe you would want to choose something different for your anthem—Gloria Gaynor's "I Will Survive" has got to be up there for many people. But, for me, the healing has been felt most through listening to what I call my "moody music". This can be music of all sorts of different genres. The main thing, though, is that it helps put me in touch with my emotions, especially my sad emotions, ironically. So, although the odd more invigorating one slips in there sometimes, it tends to be wistful cellos rather than frantic violins that I tune into; soulful harmonicas rather than strident trumpets.[7] You may not hear a great deal of cello or harmonica, but Peter Gabriel's eponymous first solo album is certainly worth a listen. Much of the album (especially side two, for those still on vinyl) seems to be anticipating some kind of cataclysmic event, but in a fearless "bring it on" kind of way, which somehow resonates with me. Listening now to songs such as "Waiting for the Big One" and "Here Comes the Flood" helps remind me of a strange, intuitive perception that I had felt for some time: a sense that I might have to cope with my own "Big One" one day, a crisis to beat all crises. When the Biggy did come, a friend who I don't think had ever suffered from clinical depression herself was still able to empathise with what was happening to me. She said "I feel as though I could have that in me too", and I knew what she meant, as I think it had always been lying dormant in me, waiting to be triggered by some catalyst at some point.

As it turns out, this isn't the end but the beginning. You see, when you fall over the Edge, you don't fall into the abyss; you fall onto the bottom. Or you could say that you have arrived at the foundations of your life again. This is also a training ground—a place where you are going to have to leave behind the things that have been undone by your breakdown, and where you will start learning new things, the things that you will need for your onward journey. Although it seems such a wretched place to be just now, it will become more bearable—I promise. In fact, you will come to realise that it has much more going for it than the cliff edge from which you have been dangling for the past few months, or years even.

We tend to view a crisis in purely negative terms, but one dictionary definition is "a decisive moment", and people's experience suggests that such times can prove to be immensely transformative. As John F. Kennedy once pointed out, the Chinese use two brush strokes to write the word "crisis". One brush stroke stands for danger; the other for opportunity. In Hippocratic thought, a crisis was certainly seen as a decisive turning point in medical terms, when the patient could expect their disease to either intensify or diminish. Without the crisis, the level of medical intervention needed to bring about ultimate healing would never be triggered. And only through the crisis would the patient's own natural healing processes be called upon to produce their maximum effect.

Conversion experiences can often come as part of a deep, personal crisis. The Greek word *metanoia*, which appears in the gospels and tends to be translated as "repentance", itself denotes a powerful experience from which a profound sense of personal and positive change can emerge. Interestingly, the word *metanoia* was also used by psychologist Carl Jung as a term to describe the process where the psyche attempts to heal itself by melting down and then being reborn in a more adaptive form. Henri Nouwen, when looking back at the pages of the spiritual journal he kept during a major depressive episode, wrote:

> Reading them now, eight years later, makes me aware of the radical changes I have undergone. I have moved from anguish to freedom, through depression to peace, through despair to hope. It certainly was a time for purification for me. My heart, ever questioning my goodness, value, and worth, has become anchored in a deeper love and thus less dependent on the praise and blame of those around me. It also has grown into a great ability to give love without always expecting love in return . . . What once seemed such a curse has become a blessing. All the agony that threatened to destroy my life now seems like the fertile ground for greater trust, stronger hope, and deeper love.[8]

And so I suppose I can understand why a therapist once told me that I should view depression as a "gift". The comment didn't go down particularly well at the time, and I certainly don't expect you to be able to see your illness in those terms if you are still in the depths of it. Indeed, the danger in talking in terms of opportunities and gifts is that we can start to romanticise depression. There have even been times in history where depression has almost obtained cult-like status, seen as something that must be endured in order to develop a certain level of creative insight (although I can't help thinking that the form of the illness being glorified must have been a different, and more bearable, form than mine). We don't want to fall into the trap of forgetting that, first and foremost, we are dealing here with an illness, and a particularly pernicious one at that. It is worth remembering that St Paul, whilst able to recognise God's purpose in his suffering of the mysterious "thorn in his side", still described whatever anguish or pain he was going through as a messenger sent from Satan (2 Corinthians 12:7).

What I think we can say with some confidence, however, is that this crisis will prove to be a make-or-break time. Mercifully, the testimony of countless sufferers of clinical depression is that it is possible to come through this thing, and for the better. It's going to require courage, discernment and wisdom to determine what is needed to restore you to health. But for now, we simply need to hang on to God's promise that he wants to work this out for your good.

And yet, we cannot help but ask: if this is indeed a "gift", why has it been given to us? We certainly didn't ask for it. And how come the vast majority of the people around us seem to get through life dealing with plenty of difficult stuff, without falling ill like this? The "why did this happen to me?" questions are always tough. They are unavoidable and perfectly natural, if not always healthy to dwell on. Ultimately, the answers are going to be complex and multi-layered, and sometimes we are just going to need patience to wait for insight to come. But one observation that I would throw out at this stage concerns the personality types of a significant number of sufferers of depressive illness. I should stress first that the people with the personality types I have in mind certainly do not have the monopoly on depressive illness. I certainly would not want anyone to feel alienated if they cannot identify with the personalities we are about to discuss; it's just that, because of their high profile amongst sufferers, I think it is worth our devoting a little time to thinking about them. We are talking about people like Rachel Kelly, a former journalist with *The Times*. In Kelly's memoir of depression, she includes a letter written by her husband, Sebastian. I must say that when I read the following extract I had an instant lump in my throat.

> When you were first ill we had your family doctor visit. He recalled a lovely memory of you as a child. You cried and cried after reading *Tarka the Otter*. I think we all cried. But you cried all night and you were still crying the next day and your mother was so concerned that she took you off to see the doctor. So maybe you were always pretty sensitive. But nothing could have prepared us for the real thing when we tried to do it all.[9]

Perhaps, like me, you can relate to this and can recall situations and events in your life that evoked strong, almost irrational, feelings against which you could do very little. Perhaps you also "get" this comment by—I am not worthy (sorry, major fan)—Kate Bush: "I wasn't an easy, happy-go-lucky girl, because I used to think about everything so much and I think I probably still do."[10] Sometimes we might wish that we could feel more indifferent about things. But deep down we know that's just not how we work. Things get under our skin. We feel the power of conviction. Ours is an intense life, and unfortunately this intensity can sometimes spill over into feelings of being overwhelmed and stressed. We can be prone to bottling things up, but if we are experiencing such uncomfortable feelings, they will only be exacerbated if we try to suppress them. In the meantime, because we can be quite private people, we may be likely to delay before asking for professional help. It sounds like a perfect storm.

The whole study of personality types is fascinating, even though I suspect there is danger in putting the theories on too high a pedestal, especially if we are to remain faithful to the Christian understanding of human personality as being unique to each and every person, and ultimately something of a mystery (in the same way as is the personhood of God, in whose image we are made). Analysing personality types, albeit on a fairly superficial level, certainly seems ubiquitous in the business world at the moment; it seems to be viewed as something of a panacea for helping teams work more "smartly" and ultimately become more profitable. There are several different models that are used today by psychologists, but the subject was really pioneered towards the end of the twentieth century by two American women, Katherine Briggs and her daughter Isabel Myers, building on the work of Jung, who in his 1921 book *Psychological Types* explored human differences of personality in terms of preferences of thought and behaviour. In Myers-Briggs terms, the people that I have been describing above as being potentially more prone to depressive illness are those who prefer to use *Feeling* and their highly developed sense of *Intuition* when processing their experience of the world. They may also be more likely to be *Introverts* than *Extraverts*. "Idealists", "Diplomats", "Mentors", "Healers" and "Counsellors" are some of the different names used by psychologists when describing people that fall within this range of personality types.

Some of the characteristics that tend to go with these kinds of personality, such as an awareness of other people's feelings and the ability to empathise with others, could be said to be attributes that all Christians might want to cultivate as part of a Christ-like character. Anecdotal evidence has led me to wonder whether there may be a disproportionately high number of Christians for whom these traits already come naturally—that is, as it were, by means of common, rather than any special, grace. I have similarly wondered whether a disproportionately high number of Christians might suffer from depressive illness. In any event, Christians with these characteristics should recognise them as having the potential for much good; it's just that I think we need to be mindful that they can also prove to be an Achilles' heel.

Sufferers of depression will often say that when they meet other sufferers they find them to be really nice, kind people. I wonder whether, as like-minded people, typically, that just means that they view them in the same positive light that they tend to view themselves! More seriously, the psychiatrist Dr Tim Cantopher suggests that there is indeed a causal link between a person's moral character and their vulnerability to depressive illness. In his book *Depressive Illness*, Cantopher explains that he doesn't bother making enquiries into a new patient's personality "because it is nearly always the same".[11] He lists the common personality characteristics of sufferers as including moral strength, reliability, diligence, a strong conscience, a strong sense of responsibility, and sensitivity. In Cantopher's experience, his patients are the sort of people "you can trust with your life". This might explain the sub-title of his book: *The curse of the strong*.

Life can be challenging enough for sensitive people trying to make sense of a world apparently dominated by ultra-confident extraverts. Jesus's claim that the meek are blessed was intended to be counter-cultural when he said it. But, in our age, perhaps more than in any previous, it is those who strive and don't let anything get in their way who are considered to be the real blessed. Don't be fooled by the antics in the TV programme *The*

Apprentice; the programme's success is due in large part to the popularity of the go-getting, enterprising role model that the contestants represent, even though in somewhat parodied form. By comparison, it is not that difficult to see why the person suffering from depression, who cannot engage in the cut and thrust and is, instead, having to sit things out on the bench, can be viewed as something of a failure by society. It is important to note here that great strides have been made in recent years to reduce the stigma associated with depressive illness, mainly by encouraging an atmosphere of increased openness in the way we discuss depression and tackle ways to treat it. I was pleased recently to see that a local mental health charity had been selected to be given one of those clear plastic receptacles of green tokens in a supermarket near to where we live. But I still felt disappointed that their box was trailing way back in third place behind the other two charities (I managed to resist the temptation to prise the boxes open to achieve a fairer distribution of the tokens). The stigma still remains, even though the prejudice can be so subtle sometimes—we might detect it lurking in a comment or reference, but will often have to unpack things a bit in order to fully expose the sentiment. For example, this is Andrew Rawnsley writing in *The Observer* about whether Ed Miliband was too "weird" to win the 2015 general election:

> But [Ed] would be no odder as prime minister than a lot of other people who have ruled Britain.

Winston Churchill saved his country—between
bouts of depression he called "the black dog"
and gargantuan consumption of alcohol. He
was a great man, but he'd not be my definition
of normal.[12]

Alright, I accept that having a drink problem may not be
a good attribute for a world leader. But I find something
unnerving in the use of the word "normal" to exclude
someone suffering from depression. Am I being over-
sensitive? I don't think so. The same stigma explains why
in 2009 Prime Minister Gordon Brown was so quick to
firmly deny the (false) rumours circulating that he was
taking MAOI–type antidepressants. There's a part of
me that thinks, who wants to be "normal", anyway? Let
them get on with it. But then there's a part of me that
thinks that no-one should be excluded from positions
of influence purely on account of having suffered mental
illness. It is important that people who are in public life
stand up and speak the truth about their own experience
of depression, and thankfully there are more and more
who do. For example, a huge "hats off" to those MPs who
in June 2012 talked so openly in the House of Commons
about such issues.[13]

Is there possibly a different type of stigma that exists
sometimes within Christian circles? It can be tempting
to wonder whether life has got on top of the Christian
suffering from depression because they didn't pray
more, or because they didn't trust God when things got

tough. It is sometimes hard for people to grasp that the individual hasn't brought the depression upon him or herself, but that the depression has *happened to them*. The way we deal with depression in our intercessory prayers in church can be revealing. I confess I felt a little frustrated when I heard prayers said for those in the congregation who were "sick", followed by prayers for those who were "depressed"; the implication being that the depressed are not sick, but could still do with being prayed for—that they might cheer up, perhaps? Or am I being over-sensitive again? Or just sensitive? And we've decided that isn't a bad thing, right?

Indeed, we need sensitive people in every walk of life. Jesus, after all, was an incredibly sensitive person. When he saw the crowds, he had compassion for them; the verb in Matthew 9:36 is, literally, to have a "gut reaction"—feelings and intuition combined. He also knew times of great anxiety; we read in Luke's Gospel that his sweat became like drops of blood whilst fervently praying in anticipation of his impending crucifixion.[14] But he also demonstrated an attractive resilience that somehow remained authentic and true to his sensitive nature. Not just a "thick skin". I believe that whilst we should be quick to affirm sensitivity, we should be aware of the benefits of developing a degree of emotional resilience, both in ourselves and in others for whom we have responsibility. We should also remember that there is strong evidence that there can be an inherited element to depression, this being the consequence of a complex interplay of genetics and environment. I am not wanting to promote any kind of cotton-wool wrapping of our loved ones, but if, say, we had a parent who suffered from anxiety or depression, it may still be sensible to consider whether there might be a familial vulnerability there and to put some kind of measures in place to try and reduce the risk of stress having an impact on the lives of other family members. There is similar wisdom in what Archbishop Justin Welby has been quoted as saying about choosing not to drink any alcohol on his own, aware that his own father suffered from a drink problem.[15] I think being realistic about the weaknesses and limitations of our personalities in this way is probably healthy. Could we even see such self-honesty as being part of the sitting-down-and-figuring-the-cost exercise that Jesus recommends each of us undertake as part of our life of Christian discipleship?[16] If we do perceive that we are lacking some emotional or mental resilience, then let's ask God to help us in that department. For example, maybe we need to seek guidance about how we should preserve our energy for what God might be calling us to do. Are there things we need to give up at work, or maybe at church? Are we trying to "do it all"?

But maybe that's for later. For now, remember, we are still lying at the bottom of the ravine, staring at the height from which we have fallen, unable even to get up. So, what next?

3. HELP

I lift up my eyes to the mountains—
where does my help come from?
Psalm 121

It might be good to remain in this supine position just a little longer, so that we can take the opportunity to contemplate an important question. That is, how should we approach this whole idea of getting better? Or, where *does* my help come from? We all know the answer to the latter question. Our help comes from God, right? Just as the psalmist immediately goes on to declare. But somehow, at this time, when we feel more in need of God than ever before, these words sound a bit like a textbook answer, and our instinct tells us that textbook answers on their own just won't do.

If we are *really* going to put our trust in God to get us out of this, what is it going to look like, feel like? St Ignatius of Loyola wrote that "there are very few people who realise what God would make of them if they abandoned themselves into his hands." I suppose a large proportion of people have never faced real back-against-the-wall

situations in their lives, particularly in the privileged
West. That might have been true of us too. Until now.
Trusting in our own ability has always been open to us,
and that is the option we have naturally chosen, even
when, let's be honest, we have tried to cover it with a kind
of prayerful veneer. There is also a natural inclination in
most of us to avoid unnecessary risk or change. But if
we have allowed this to have free reign, it may have led
us to becoming too cushioned, too cosy, too insulated.
I remember watching a TV programme that featured
an outdoors enthusiast who loved to go running in the
hills and mountains in all conditions, but especially in
the ice and snow. He didn't take a map with him, nor a
compass, nor a mobile phone, because what gave him
real joy whilst he was out running in the remotest of
parts was the sense of having to trust God to guide him
and bring him home safely. My moderately risk-averse
wife was watching with me and thought that this was
foolhardiness in the extreme. But I wonder whether
maybe that guy had a point. If we really do want to put
our faith in God, then maybe we should actually be
looking for opportunities to experience and know how
that feels. I'm not sure whether this is a good example or
not, but I used to be an incredibly nervous flyer, and now
I actually look forward to take-offs and landings, almost
seeing them as a visual aid for wanting to trust God for
all the ups and downs of life. I think what I am talking
about is different to the sort of putting-God-to-the-test
which the Bible warns against, and certainly seems more

edifying than putting our efforts into ensuring a risk-free existence for ourselves. "Those who try to make their life secure will lose it, but those who lose their life will keep it."[17] These words of Jesus, even when admittedly taken out of context, seem to find an application here. Maybe we will have to start letting go of things and putting ourselves out there more, even if we don't yet have the energy to go fell-running. It makes me think of some advice given by God (played by Morgan Freeman) in the film *Evan Almighty*:

> Let me ask you something. If someone prays for patience, you think God gives them patience? Or does he give them *the opportunity* to be patient? If he prayed for courage, does God give him courage, or does he give him *opportunities* to be courageous? If someone prayed for the family to be closer, do you think God zaps them with warm fuzzy feelings, or does he give them *opportunities* to love each other?[18]

Or to take another movie, think of Dorothy and her friends as they go in search of the Wizard of Oz, hoping that he will give them the gifts they desperately long for. As a kid I used to feel generally unimpressed by the cowardly Wizard, later revealed by Toto as something of a fraud. But I now wonder whether he was doing more than just buying time when he set the characters the task of bringing back the wicked witch's broomstick. Maybe he was showing great wisdom, knowing that it would only be in that treacherous task's completion that these comrades would develop the characteristics that they had been seeking from him in the first place.

Perhaps if we are honest, the petitioning of a fabled wizard may not be a million miles from how sometimes we approach God. If, having dared bring up the subject of our illness in prayer, we do not receive a more tangible and obvious form of healing from God, this can rock us. Or sometimes we can live our lives with an unchallenged assumption that we probably aren't one of the lucky ones who are able to tap into God's healing power anyway. Rather than being distracted by such hang-ups, we would probably do better by finding out where the healing is already taking place in our lives—yes, it is there, somewhere!—and trying to be thankful for this. I know that we can also get unstuck by not understanding how asking for God's help will fit in with the medical treatment that we have been advised to follow. We are not in a position to doubt the validity of their claims, but, still, we might not be helped by hearing the testimonies of those who have claimed instant healing from God. These people tell us that they immediately threw all their antidepressants in the bin, and the suggestion seems to be that they should never have been relying on medication in the first place. As I write, there have been some controversies in other fields of medicine where doctors have reported patients saying that they have been told by their church leaders not to continue with their medication, and instead to trust in the healing power of God. We might feel uncomfortable about that sort of thing, but how do we personally reconcile our faith in conventional medicine—including psychiatric medicine—with our belief in God's healing activity?

I had always wondered what Christians meant when they referred to Jesus as being the "Great Physician". When my own back was against the wall, and as a few pennies started to drop, I found myself able to understand God as somehow overseeing the recovery process and guiding me on what felt like a path of growth and healing. I could see that this involved putting me in touch with the right people in the fields of psychiatry and psychology, and giving me discernment when different options in terms of treatment or medical advice presented themselves. Of course I have taken numerous wrong turns. These have often left me railing at God and beating myself up at the same time. But when the dust has settled and the ranting has subsided, I have reflected, and tried to see whether the crisis might have involved my running before I could walk, or if I had been driving my recovery, as opposed to letting myself be drawn or guided. I am also aware that a big obstacle in seeking God's help has been my struggle at times to accept the reality and seriousness of the illness. It actually took me a long time to appreciate that I was really unwell from a neurochemical point of view. This was in part due to sheer denial, and in part due to a degree of ignorance about the illness. But also in the mix was some rather Pharisaic thinking: the thought that

I was somehow above suffering from clinical depression. The stigma within, I suppose. In addition, I was able to recall one or two "wobbles" in the past (which now seem like mild gusts of wind compared to the force ten gale that was to be the Big One) and I had somehow managed to get over those without any medical intervention. I probably hoped that whatever I was experiencing might similarly pass of its own accord.

I once heard a speaker at a Christian conference say that a precondition of receiving any form of healing by God is that we are completely honest before him—honest about our emotions and the facts concerning our predicament. Although we might fear such honesty, in the end it turns out to be liberating. In his book *God of Surprises*, Gerard Hughes reassures us that, in all things, "the facts are kind", because "God is in the facts".[19] If we let this idea sink in, beyond the textbook-answer level that is, we may start to truly appreciate, for the first time, that there is *nothing* about our situation God doesn't know about or cannot work through. We need not fear reality. God has seen it all before, but he also sees it and even experiences it now, in the context of our own unique circumstances. Rowan Williams recognises a similar theme in the wisdom of the desert fathers in *Silence and Honeycakes*. He quotes the somewhat peculiar-sounding advice of a nameless elder to a brother struggling with temptation: "Go. Sit in your cell and give your body in pledge to the walls." The idea is that we have to avoid the temptation to flee from whatever is causing us distress.

Applying the same wisdom to our own circumstances, we learn it is only by remaining committed to experiencing what is actually happening to us, to "espousing reality rather than unreality", that we will eventually find flourishing and freedom. In fact, it is a "rather startling intensification of the command to love yourself".[20] We owe it to ourselves, you could say. Furthermore, and quoting Gerard Hughes again, we need to trust that, to some extent at least, "the answer is *in the pain*".[21] Yes, the very pain that seems to want to destroy us is where we need to bide a while. No running away. Indeed, if only we would let him, we will find that Christ *"shares our pain, absorbs it, and offers his peace in return".*[22]

This can all feel so counterintuitive that we will probably have to persevere for a while. Part of the discipline will involve recognising the ultimately unhelpful voice of our ego telling us to redouble our efforts and not let the side down. "You're not going to achieve much pledging yourself to the walls", it hollers. Our ego has itself been wounded by our illness and is in self-admonishing overdrive, believing this is the best way to get us to pull our socks up. We may feel guilty about what has happened to us, but the guilt is false. Have you ever seen that very moving, poignant scene in the movie *Good Will Hunting*, the one where the therapist (played by Robin Williams) repeatedly tells Will (Matt Damon), "it's not your fault"?[23] He repeats it again and again, eyeball to eyeball, until Will eventually gives in and breaks down in tears. Well, it's not your fault. If anyone has a problem, it is those who cannot see that no-one would have ever asked this to happen to them. As Alastair Campbell wryly tweeted when there was a lot of commentary about Stephen Fry's own battle with depression: "To those asking what @stephenfry has to be depressed about, would you ask what someone has to be cancerous, diabetic or asthmatic about?"[24]

Taking time to think about these things can help us understand our situation better and what it might mean to receive help and healing from God. But however life-giving the insights we receive during our recovery from illness are, and however important it is to learn how to suffer well, the pain of our illness is going to be too excruciating for us to bear at times, especially in the early weeks or months. When things are at their worst like this, I don't think God wants us to endure being in that place of pain and agony for any considerable period of time, if we can avoid it. We should be seeking medical assistance, just as anyone suffering from cancer, diabetes or asthma would do. This is what we will look at in the next chapter.

4. MY BRAIN HURTS

Is there no balm in Gilead? Is there no physician there?
Jeremiah 8:22

When one of my colleagues found out that I was suffering from depression, he told me that when he had been a trainee solicitor, one of his fellow trainees had ended up having to quit their law firm on account of the illness. This poor person had apparently explained to his friends that his depression had been caused by a chemical imbalance in his brain. I remember thinking that this must have been something really serious—chemical imbalance in the brain? Wow! Now, I suppose we could have a chicken-or-egg debate about whether a neurochemical imbalance *causes* clinical depression, or whether it is the triggering of the depressed state that causes the imbalance; but this wasn't the reason why I somehow did not connect my illness with that story when I first heard it. I have already mentioned that it took me a long time to fully appreciate that what I was suffering from was a real, diagnosable, illness. I have also explained that I think the reasons for this were partly linked to my own previous skirmishes with mental illness and my ability to ride those out somehow. But I was mainly just plain ignorant. And not having a degree in neurochemistry, or knowing anyone who had suffered from depression, I suppose this was not surprising, and so I will try and refrain from beating myself up about it.

The decision to prescribe psychoactive medication is a fairly significant one, and the over-prescription of antidepressants, particularly in cases of milder depression, has gained wide coverage in the media. I certainly did not raise any questions when the GP prescribed me Citalopram. But I was in meltdown and not really in a position to do anything other than follow the professional advice. Later on, however, and once I was feeling a bit better—maybe three or four months down the line—I began to wonder if the Citalopram could be part of the problem rather than the solution. Perhaps the medication was why I still often couldn't sleep at night, and still didn't feel like "me"? I was also influenced by comments from those around me, such as "you don't *look* clinically depressed", which made me question whether I needed to be on medication at all. I also remembered people saying that antidepressants often mask the real problem and can be an obstacle to addressing the real issues that led to the onset of depression. To the extent that I was feeling better, I began to suspect that this was in spite of the drugs I was taking, rather than thanks to them.

In any event, and having discussed it with my GP first, I gradually weaned myself off the medication. And, initially, I seemed to feel much better for it. However, within five months or so, with work becoming busier again and most of my normal extra-curricular activities resumed, I was flat on my back, staring upwards at the same cliff that I had fallen from earlier. What had happened? Most likely, the initial major depressive episode had mainly gone into remission—perhaps due in part to the passing of time, perhaps assisted to some extent by the Citalopram—but I was still prone to relapses, which were mainly triggered by over-exertion and stress. Eventually, this vulnerability led to the onset of another major depressive episode, which unfortunately was much worse than the first one. Would that have happened had I stayed on the Citalopram? I'll never know.

By the time of this second "breakdown" (an unfashionable term, but that's how it felt), I had been advised by a psychologist whom I had started to see that I really ought to seek the specialist help of a consultant psychiatrist. This would have to be arranged privately if I wanted to see the specialist quickly. I had been reluctant to go down the "medical route" again but, as with the previous crisis, it seemed that I wasn't really in much of a position to do otherwise than follow the professional advice.

The psychiatrist began by prescribing a similar type of medication to the Citalopram—this time it was Sertraline, which is another drug in the family of antidepressants known as "SSRIs". SSRIs are one of the more modern types of antidepressants and are promoted for first-line use by GPs, not least because they have less onerous side effects than some of the other forms of medication. SSRI stands for "selective serotonin re-uptake inhibitor", denoting that the medication is designed to increase the concentration of the neurotransmitter in the brain known as serotonin. Neurotransmitters are the chemicals that direct the workings of the central nervous system, and serotonin is a neurotransmitter which is responsible for many of our "positive feelings", including a sense of well-being, confidence and self-esteem. It is also needed to obtain deep and restful sleep. The SSRIs work by (ultimately) reducing the activity of the receptors in our nerve cells which would normally soak up serotonin, thus leaving more serotonin circulating around the brain.

And so this is why I should have really been able to connect with my colleague's story of the trainee solicitor. When people suffer from clinical depression, there is an imbalance of certain neurotransmitters in their brain. Or perhaps it is better to understand the neurotransmitters which you need to be doing their job as moving too sluggishly. The more severe the depression, the more sluggish the neurotransmitters. For me, despite the scientific explanations, any talk of neurotransmitters still conjures up images of little cartoon characters inside the control centre of someone's brain, a bit like the Numskulls—*Beezer* or *Beano* readers will understand—each tasked with various functions such as "make him happy" or "make him nervous". Once depression takes a hold, less friendly types of Numskulls—nothing like the ones from the comic strip—suddenly appear on the scene.

And suddenly, they are at the helm, shouting at the top of their tiny voices, "Make him feel the most wretched he could ever imagine possible."

Unfortunately, as with the Citalopram, but now on an even greater scale, the Sertraline medication seemed to augment my anxiety symptoms, making me feel unpleasantly "wired". This is a well-recognised side effect of SSRIs; the flooding of serotonin in the brain actually triggers an initial throttling back of serotonin production—hence the increased anxiety, which only decreases once the body adapts by lowering the sensitivity and activity of the receptors. For most patients, this side effect should only last the first couple of weeks of being on the medication, with things settling down by three to four weeks (indeed, it is worth mentioning that one should normally wait until around four weeks of being on any type of anti-depressant medication before expecting to recognise any benefits). However, even allowing for these lead-in times, in a minority of patients (yours truly included), the often unbearable symptoms persist and the SSRIs just do not seem to be doing the business. In my case, the psychiatrist introduced a different antidepressant, Dosulepin, which belongs to an older family of antidepressants first used in the 1950s, known as the "tricyclics" (or "TCAs"). These are named after their chemical structure, which includes three rings of atoms. Among other effects, TCAs are understood to keep the brain supplied not only with serotonin, but also with another neurotransmitter, noradrenaline (known as norepinephrine in the US).

Noradrenaline is associated with making us feel alert and energised—a "gas pedal" chemical.[25] If someone had been able to install a noradrenaline-gauge in my brain, I think I must have gone beyond the red zone when I was in the depths of the illness. I can still recall those terrifying times—they probably each lasted minutes, but they felt like hours—when I remained physically frozen, not able to do anything other than wait for the stupor to lift.

Equipped with this kindergarten level of understanding of how brain chemistry works, I can now (sort of) understand why the new medication worked better for me. Sure, I was low in serotonin, but I was also low in noradrenaline, and probably dopamine (another gas-pedal chemical) as well. As it happens, some experts say that TCAs can often be more effective than SSRIs in the treatment of a sub-type of depression which is sometimes referred to as melancholic depression, many of the symptoms of which seemed to correspond with what I had. Sleeplessness is a common symptom of depression, and in this regard TCAs have an added advantage of having a sedative effect, which is why they tend to be taken at night.

I pause here at the mention of sleep, as I still have a somewhat uneasy relationship with it. A friend once described sleep as a bit like the reset button on an electronic device. Whatever sort of day you've had, you'll normally feel better after a night's sleep, right? Well I lost my reset button, and without it, the pain I was going through was exacerbated beyond measure. I also pause at the mention of the word "sleeplessness", because how that word is commonly used means nothing compared to what I went through. And I pause because I know my skills are limited in being able to describe the hell—and I don't use that word lightly—that I endured on account of the sleep deprivation associated with my illness. I'm sorry, but I don't think I can venture much beyond that, at least not now. That sounds as though I'm welching out. It's weird, as I thought I had more to share on this subject—I had plans to devote a whole chapter to it—but it seems as though I am not ready yet. But perhaps there is a bit of advice I could offer. I should first agree that it will be useful and positive to learn during your recovery about how practising "sleep hygiene" can help promote the sleep function that you once took for granted. I also accept that in certain circumstances it will be appropriate to take medication to help you sleep (although watch out for the hangover effect the following day). But these things won't really address the issue. The issue is that your brain chemistry has changed, an effect of which is that your sleep function no longer works properly. Therefore, don't think that if only you could sleep you would suddenly feel better. Remember, you are poorly and need to be made well again—only then will the sleep function start to return to normal.

Following on from the point I was making about different types of medication being used to address different symptoms in depression, we may find it helpful

to understand why different people should experience
different symptoms in the first place.

As I have already mentioned,[26] the International Classification of Diseases and Related Health Problems,
devised by the World Health Organisation and currently
on its tenth revision (ICD-10), contains a diagnosis of
"Depressive Episode", subdivided into "Mild depressive
episode", "Moderate depressive episode" and "Severe
depressive episode" (the latter with or without psychotic
symptoms). The differentiation between the diagnoses
is said to rest "upon a complicated clinical judgement
that involves the number, type, and severity of symptoms
present. The extent of ordinary social and work activities is often a useful general guide to the likely degree
of severity of the episode." At one point, my thirst for
answers (and a diagnosis that seemed more specific to my
symptoms) led me to read some of the material produced
by the pioneering Black Dog Institute in New South
Wales, Australia (I would certainly recommend a visit to
their website). The institute's model for treating depression (or "the depressions") involves assessing whether
the patient is suffering from "Psychotic", "Melancholic"
or "Non-Melancholic" depression and recommending
therapies best suited to the type of depression diagnosed.
Having said that, I am also aware that similar categories
of depression were popular in psychiatric practice and
research in the UK in the 1980s but are no longer used.

In terms of prognosis, a depressive episode, once in
remission, may or may not leave residual symptoms.

Outcomes depend on factors such as the severity of the episode and whether or not the patient has already suffered a previous episode. Also, the better the treatment that the patient receives, the less likely it is for the patient to be left with residual symptoms, and the risk of a relapse (of the first episode) or a recurrence (by way of a second episode) is reduced. In cases where the patient is considered to be at particular risk of relapse or recurrence, long-term management by way of medication is recommended.

ICD-10 also refers to "Persistent mood [affective] disorders", described as "persistent and usually fluctuating disorders of mood in which individual episodes are rarely if ever sufficiently severe to warrant being described as hypomanic or even mild depressive episodes". These forms of depression can involve long lasting periods of low mood, often starting in the early life of the sufferer. Talking therapies such as psychotherapy can often prove to be more effective than medication. When a sufferer is unfortunate enough to go on and suffer from a depressive episode, this can be referred to as "double depression".

You can certainly find plenty of material out there about all of this, but remember, the internet is not always your friend. Many a time I have wished that I had resisted the temptation to search Google for something, the search usually ending up at some random chain of noticeboard discussions, which, upon reading, made me feel much worse than before. We impatiently seek answers to our questions, and if we cannot access expert advice quickly, we believe that the internet is the most likely source of instant gratification. In my experience, the better way might still be to wait for the answer, from whichever source it may come, and resist that temptation to hit the search engine. I have found that when the answer does come, it is normally accompanied by a kind of assurance, a hitting-of-the-spot, with a welcomed lightness of touch. When it comes to understanding depressive illness from a medical perspective, it probably also pays to start by reading a decent book on the subject. I have already referred to Dr Tim Cantopher's short book *Depressive Illness*, and I was grateful when a copy was kindly handed to me by a member of our church just when I really needed it.[27] At the time, I had been struggling with some references that I had come across on the internet that seemed to portray clinical depression as something which, once first suffered, would lead to a life-long battle of having to cope with successive episodes. Although I accepted that this might be the reality for some people, I was still looking for a more positive message. Then I came across this in Dr Cantopher's book:

> If you look at most textbooks on depressive illness, you will read that it is usually a recurrent condition. That is, most people who get an episode go on to have one or more further episodes in the future. *I don't find this to be so.* Whilst some people do have recurrent spells of depression, they are in two groups. The first

> group comprises those who have a recurrent illness which is independent of, and largely unaffected, by stress … The second group, which is much the larger, comprises those who get further episodes of clinical depression because they have learnt and changed nothing from their first episode.[28]

I didn't think this was necessarily saying that other sufferers still wouldn't be left with some residual symptoms, or suffer from mini-relapses or "blips" from time to time. But it did seem to allay some of my concerns about my prognosis, whilst containing a sobering challenge about the need to respond to the illness in order to minimise the risk of developing a more long-term condition. More of that later.

I hope I haven't confused you too much in this chapter. If it helps, nothing in all the books and articles I ever read seemed to really describe what I "had". I wonder if part of the problem is that we are coming up here against the uniqueness of each individual's mind, meaning that the attempt to identify more specific types of depression with corresponding treatments is always going to be more of a challenge than, say, distinguishing type 1 and type 2 diabetes in patients. Despite fully accepting the link between the chemical imbalance in a sufferer's mind and the emotional turmoil experienced during depression, I am still not sure that we can really say, "all roads lead to the neurotransmitters eventually."[29] Part of me finds it hard to accept that we can boil things down into such deterministic terms.

But that is not to say that a belief in the ultimate mystery of the human psyche must always be held in tension with the science that informs and supports psychiatric medicine. One would hope that the latter, as it develops and improves, will lead to more reliable treatments for different types of depression. Despite the great strides that have been made in psychiatry over the last few decades, many sufferers end up having to go through painful and prolonged periods of trial and error with their medication. Weeks, months, can be spent having to persevere with trialling various medications until the right one is found. What is salve to some can feel like poison to others. Some people hear the scare stories about how medication can make people feel much worse, and so are put off from seeking medical assistance in the first place.

But speaking from my own experience, I can really say that I did come to see the medication as an important part of the solution. Remarkable, really, after such a shaky start. Earlier on, I can remember panicking that the search for the right medication was going to be futile. The story of the woman in Luke 8:43 who spent all her money on physicians before finally coming to Jesus for healing came to my mind. Was that going to be me—was I going to have to give up on conventional medicine? Jesus's miracle in that story certainly contained a potent sign of the coming of his kingdom. But I don't think we should take from this that Jesus's healing power cannot be found in less dramatic forms, or that persevering with medical treatment (whether or not that involves parting with our own money) is always going to be futile. Remember, trust the Great Physician. If we had any preconceived ideas about the sort of balm that was going to make us feel better, it was probably not going to be those little pills with futuristic-sounding, high-scoring-Scrabble names. Are they really the best that Gilead can offer? Well, God can surprise us, sometimes.

5. THINKING DIFFERENTLY

It is for freedom that Christ has set us free.
Galatians 5:1

We have seen how the field of psychiatry may challenge our outlook as Christians. We may feel equally challenged when it comes to considering the various forms of counselling and psychotherapy that are on offer. We will certainly be advised by medical practitioners to look into the "talking therapies", and my view is that we are probably going to need their assistance, if our minds are going to recover from the ravages of depressive illness. Reading books about the theories and principles behind this stuff can be hugely beneficial (OK, I would say that), but they only take you so far. And now is probably a good time to consider therapy—if you are off the floor again, by which I mean your condition has improved a little since the initial breakdown. Any improvement might be due, in part, to getting some proper rest; it may also be that any medication that you have been prescribed has started to "kick in". You will still be in a fragile state, but

you may feel up to starting the process of talking about
what has happened to you, how awful it still feels, what
can be done to make it feel better, and how you can help
to prevent it happening again.

I think some of my own scepticism about therapists
was to do with wanting to protect the inner world of my
"Christian psyche", this being the place where prayers
were formed and experiences of God drawing near were
felt. And I suppose I was aware of Jesus's own teaching,
which made it clear that inner thoughts and feelings could
be just as morally reprehensible as outward actions. This
was sacred, but also potentially dangerous territory, and
I was reluctant to let practitioners loose on it, especially
secular ones. Wasn't Sigmund Freud a bit of an atheist
poster boy?

I recently found an old copy of *The Shattered Mirror*,
by Christian psychiatrist John White, at the back of our
bookshelf; according to the date I had written on the
inside cover, I must have read this in my final year as a law
undergraduate. Possibly its influence was still felt when I
was trying to cope with my breakdown some seventeen
years later. One of the theses of the book is that therapy
as a means to resolving someone's mental turmoil is never
going to be enough (that is religion's role), and it can even
make things worse. Psychotherapy shouldn't try to mess
with religion, nor religion with psychotherapy. Perhaps
White's own experience of medical training helps explain
his views concerning this great divide:

> I was taught as a resident in psychiatry that I must
> never allow a patient to talk to me about religion.
> The reason? Discussions of religion raised by
> patients usually represented a resistance to the
> psychotherapeutic process. Religious themes
> were antitherapeutic. They were the client's
> escape route from the medicine of the therapist.[30]

But when it came to it, when I really had to cope with
the Big One, such doubts and concerns didn't seem to
pass muster. Maybe I was just feeling desperate and was
prepared to grab hold of anything that offered succour.
But also, the theoretical objections to therapy suddenly
seemed to be based more on fear than in love. And so,
despite still having considerable reservations, I decided
that I would give it a go.

It seems modern people have no difficulty appreciating
that the mind, that part of us which is capable of thought,
transcends the physical organ that we call our brain. What
they do not easily recognise—and I think I had fallen
into this trap—is that our mind is something different
to the parts of us which the Bible describes as spirit, or
soul. We either ignore these other aspects of ourselves,
or conflate them with the mind. Either way, the mind
ends up being elevated, to the detriment of our spiritual
life. Or as John Main puts it: "As a result, [modern man]
has lost that sense of his own balance and proportion as
a creature which should lead him into the creative silence
of prayer."[31] Maybe another effect of the elevation of the

mind is that we can end up living our lives as if the mind is something to which we are subservient, and so we may lose the will to challenge many of the thoughts, images and ideas that our minds conjure up on a daily basis. It has certainly been ground-breaking for me to appreciate that my mind flourishes best when it is not given free rein. Living from this new dynamic, I learn that I can confront my mind with compassion and without fear.

Personality is an incredibly difficult, abstract concept. But it is one that the sufferer of depression may feel forced to grapple with, because they suddenly find that their own personality, something which they previously took for granted, has become so fragmented and distorted. I think it is common in people whose minds break down to want to rediscover and then cling on to the irreducible core of their being, what we might want to call "the real me", in a new and powerful way. This is not the self-serving ego we are talking about, but the part of me which, whenever glimpsed, makes me feel free and open; the part of me where I sense a sort of home-coming, and which I am more aware of in times of prayer and spiritual insight. It is worth remembering that we are not talking about looking for a sort of inner-enlightenment, but rather a re-connection with what Margaret Silf describes as our "Who Centre".[32] Although we realise that this Who Centre has been overlooked in the daily grind of our lives, we are utterly relieved to find that it has not left us, that it has not been destroyed by the depression. I think sufferers of depression often have an intuitive sense that part of their escape route will involve having to connect with their Who Centre at a deeper level than ever before. This is something that can be, literally, life and death—don't confuse it with the seemingly selfish pursuit which people sometimes describe as "finding themselves". And because this deepest part of their personality does in fact connect them with the spiritual domain—being the part that is closest to God—it is perhaps no surprise that sufferers of depression end up seeking spiritual answers to life's questions, even if they started out as people of no particular faith. Why more of them seem to look to Buddhism than Christianity is a fascinating question, although probably beyond the scope of this book.

I have talked about how we might want to jealously guard our Christian identity (certainly not a bad thing), and perhaps this is why Christians are likely to feel more strongly that their counsellor or psychotherapist, rather than, say, their dentist or chiropodist, should also be a Christian. As it happened, my first therapy-encounter was with a Christian counsellor (I had deliberately chosen him on account of his being one). It turned out to be spectacularly disastrous—I ended up walking out. He talked and talked, telling me various anecdotes and stories from his difficult past, and I just could not cope with hearing this. Looking back, I was probably too unwell to go to that first session. But, still, my experience shows that there is no guarantee that by seeking out a Christian a counsellor or therapist (or indeed a Christian dentist or chiropodist), we will get the right help. I think the important thing to remember is that we are not looking to therapy for any new belief system that might replace our own faith. Yes, we will need to keep our antennae out for anything that we feel conflicts with our beliefs, but I think we can be reasonably confident that the therapist's main aim will be to help our mind function more normally again, and not to threaten our values. One of the most important criteria is that you actually get on with the therapist and that you respect him or her (you could be spending quite a bit of time together talking about some pretty personal stuff). Personal recommendations can be so valuable here, so if you know people that have had therapy, ask them who they have used and how they rated them. You may also find it useful to check out resources such as www.counselling-directory.org.uk to help you locate a therapist who suits your own particular needs.

But how will we know what form of therapy is going to be best for us? Just as with medical treatments for depression, I certainly think we should be wary of a one-size-fits-all approach here. A particular therapy may suit one person, but could be detrimental for someone else. We are already in a very vulnerable state, and bad therapy can be like treading on an explosive device. We might end up being stretchered off, back to the trenches, scared to raise our heads above the parapet again for weeks. So we have to be as discerning as possible when seeking out the right help, whilst appreciating that, ultimately, we take a risk whenever we approach a therapist or counsellor. Bravery isn't a bad thing to pray for.

A friend once said that CBT had, quite literally, changed his life. My friend had not been suffering from depression, but had got to a stage in his life when he realised there were issues which he needed to start thinking about, well, just, differently. When I say "thinking differently" here, I mean in the cognitive sense; that is, the processes we use to think about things, rather than the substance of what we might be thinking about. In fact, that is what the "C" in CBT stands for: "*Cognitive* Behavioural Therapy". CBT was developed by the American psychiatrist Aaron Beck in the 1960s. It is probably naivety on my part, but sometimes I wonder why it took until the 1960s for someone to come up with the theory that the way we think, the way we feel, and the way we behave are all inter-connected (and this is what CBT really boils down to). But the theory certainly works. By applying CBT to depression, the sufferer can start to understand that the painful *feelings* that are afflicting them are closely linked to, or exacerbated by, the negative *thought patterns* that are also a feature of the illness. Those thought patterns might include catastrophising (constantly thinking that the worst will happen) or always focusing on the negative. We also might find that we are plagued by invasive, obsessive thoughts. Another classic thought pattern involves fusing our thoughts with reality, or we might "buy into" our thoughts and their related memories and feelings. As the former All Black John Kirwan puts it, "negative thoughts get into your mind and grow out of all proportion, and before you know it, you're responding to your thoughts as if they were real."[33] The third corner of the CBT triangle involves understanding that our *behaviour*—for example, whether we want to engage in social activity or not—can be affected by the way we think and feel, and vice versa.

Unfortunately, our natural reactions to what we are experiencing in depression only tend to make matters worse. Our automatic response is to put all our mental energy (of which we have very little) into dispelling or neutralising our negative thoughts and emotions, or avoiding certain situations which we associate with them. And with every shovel of soil we dig, the hole that we are trying to get out of just gets bigger. We tire ourselves out and end up feeling more splintered and scattered than when we began. It is important to recognise that these distressing thoughts and emotions have their roots in fear; a form of fear that is induced by illness, but fear none the less. And we also have to remember that love trumps fear.[34] In fact, love trumps everything. I have a faithful and wise friend who once gave me the following simple advice: "There is always a way". I know that this could sound a bit pie in the sky, but I do think we are talking about a spiritual truth here; however bad things are, there is a loving, God-centred way through. There has to be. So, perhaps using some of the psychological theory we have learned, what might be the best way to respond lovingly to our turbulent thoughts and feelings? First, I believe we need to stop digging and put down our shovel. Remember the desert father's advice about pledging ourselves to the walls? Well, we need to pledge ourselves to our hole. We choose to embrace reality with all its messiness and pain, and turn away from our preconceptions of how our recovery might progress. We accept that this chaotic inner world, although it feels alien, belongs to us nonetheless. Taking ownership is liberating. We let ourselves feel what it is really like to be in the hole, whilst at the same time trusting that our thoughts and emotions are not going to overwhelm us. Remember, although it feels like we are walking through a fire, we can still come through this without being burned up in the process, with scars to prove it no doubt.[35] Changing metaphors again, we also learn to let our thoughts and emotions pass, just like a train passing through a station. Whatever weird and toxic thoughts were on board, there's no point trying to drag the train back; that would require super-human strength and, besides, there'll be another train passing soon, and you don't want to cause a collision.

We can thus seek to apply CBT techniques to arrive at a new way of thinking, to help distance and untangle ourselves from our thoughts and emotions at a time when they are proving just too much to handle. But as can hopefully be seen in the examples I have just tried to describe, it may also prove beneficial to combine a subjective awareness with our thoughts and emotions, in a way that does not compromise the objectivity with which we are trying to view them. To achieve this, psychologists and therapists alike would recommend the practice of "mindfulness". According to the proponents of mindfulness, if we spend more time being aware of things in the present, rather than focusing on the past or the future, we will become better at dealing with stressful situations and distressing feelings. We will develop a way of accepting our thoughts, rather than over-identifying with them, and our mindset will hopefully become more flexible and adaptable in the process.

I was interested to discover from a friend that a professor of psychology at Oxford and influential proponent of mindfulness is also an ordained priest in the Church of England. The renowned Professor Mark Williams, together with colleagues John D. Teasdale and Zindel Segal, has developed a therapy known as Mindfulness-based Cognitive Therapy, particularly aimed at preventing relapse and recurrence in depression.[36] I suppose my ears had pricked up because I am aware that mindfulness is normally seen as an import from Buddhist philosophy, and that some Christians, perhaps understandably, feel wary about adopting its concepts. Even as I write, the editorial in the *Church of England Newspaper* refers, in a somewhat censorious tone, to "the spread of the 'Mindfulness' Movement" as "a Buddhist movement of self-understanding and 'attentiveness' to my own self".[37] Perhaps we can detect in those words an undercurrent of disapproval of any form of meditative or contemplative practice. Maybe we might be viewed by other Christians as indulging in "me–time" if we were to choose to spend time in meditation, time that surely could be more productively used by rolling up our yoga mat, then our sleeves, and getting on with the real work. However, whilst mindfulness in Christianity does not have the same credal importance as it does in Buddhism, it seems to have pretty deep roots in Christian tradition as a spiritual discipline. Thinking again about the desert fathers, they stressed the importance of *attention* and the dangers of *inattention*; they came to appreciate that it is only in paying attention to everything, both inner and outer, that it is possible to see the world *as it really is*. That includes seeing *ourselves as* we *really are*. Many Christians through the ages have learned that by attending to our thoughts, it is possible to discern between those which help us develop a more devotional life, and those that distract our attention from the thing that we really want to focus on. Indeed, it is hard to see why living in the moment shouldn't have anything other than positive connotations. Aren't we more likely to meet God in the present, and less so when we are trudging through our memories, or dreaming, or worrying about what the future may hold?

But back to our hole, which we are still daring to let our mind experience and not run away from. Depression can certainly feel like the worst prison imaginable, but I believe our experience of it can lead us towards a new kind of freedom in the way we think. I'm not actually a huge fan of *Doctor Who*, but I have sometimes drifted in and out of episodes of *The Sarah Jane Adventures,* the spin-off series for children, which my own children enjoyed watching. One of the episodes really gripped me, and instead of drifting in and out, I remained firmly anchored to the chair throughout. One of the characters— I think he was called Clyde—had fallen under the curse of some kind of evil alien totem pole, which meant that he was suddenly seen as a mortal enemy through the eyes of all his friends. The friends felt uncomfortable about harbouring these hostile thoughts towards him, but they seemed completely trapped and unable to change anything, and it was their plight more than Clyde's that somehow grabbed my attention. Clyde was eventually saved by another friend, who, being from another planet, was not affected by the curse; she realised that the curse's power could be broken by his friends repeating Clyde's name over and over, like a mantra. And I thought; that is how it is with depression. We feel its pain, but we are powerless to do anything about it until we recognise it, name it, and start to understand it. The thoughts *feel* real—that's part of the "curse". But in moments of precious insight we start to appreciate that these thoughts and emotions are not based in truth. We learn to recognise their jagged, alien edge. And we also learn that there's no point hitting out at them, or reasoning them away; to use the beautiful language of the prayer book (admittedly out of context), we should not try to "dissemble or cloak" them. Instead, we have to trust and believe that the reason we are experiencing this distorted version of reality is because we are unwell. I found it helpful to put this slowly emerging inner conviction into words (such as "I Am Still Me!"), and then either write them in my journal or shout them out in wide open spaces. I can remember finding it particularly therapeutic, on a cycling trip through the Northumberland countryside, to cry out my mantra to the passing wildlife. It was almost an act of defiance. Whatever helps in breaking the curse, I suppose.

As we start dealing with our depression-induced thought patterns in this way, we also begin to recognise that, even before we became ill, there were certain ways of thinking and of reacting to situations that were probably unhealthy. The poverty of our old defence mechanisms now becomes fully apparent, and we come to realise just how much energy we were wasting on them. For so long, we have been fearing the unknown and clinging onto all sorts of things for security. We have forgotten how to live with uncertainty. "The wind blows wherever it pleases. You hear its sound, but you cannot tell where it comes from or where it is going. So it is with everyone born of the Spirit."[38] We might consider ourselves to be born of the Spirit, but we now realise that we have adopted a rigid approach to living that seems incompatible with this status. In our defence, there are good reasons for this. We have loved our loved ones so much, and this may have led to overprotection. *Finding Nemo* is an amazing lesson about the perils of being an overprotective parent. I remember watching it for the first time in a cinema when I was away on business. Our first child was probably less than one year old at the time. By the end of the movie I was in tears—tears of consolation, I suppose. But although the truth had certainly hit home for me that evening, the film did not prove to be an antidote to my overprotectiveness. It is during this time of being "laid low" that we have a unique opportunity to take stock of our lives, and can really commit to change. And, strangely, we find a new fearlessness developing in ourselves about what might lie ahead.

Athletes need to be as supple as possible. By using various stretching techniques, they learn to inhibit the way in which the body automatically contracts the muscles surrounding a joint when it comes under strain. And it is not dissimilar for those who are trying to restore movement to a mind that has reached breaking point. Thinking about our physical movement can help us understand our mental wellbeing in many ways. A game that I sometimes play involves catching myself when I have unconsciously started to clench my fist—in bed, at work, wherever. I then consciously relax the muscles and slowly turn the fist into an opened palm. This small act seems to release a sense of openness and freedom within both body and spirit. We need to gently coax, manipulate, our entrenched and rigid thought patterns into new, more flexible, pathways. Listen to Stephen Cherry:

> To be open, we need to have reached some kind of mastery over the subconscious perceptual filters which constantly limit our experience and render the world less frightening, but also

less interesting, challenging and vivid than it really is.[39]

Again, we come back to the idea of experiencing life as it really is. No lyric-mangling.

But we may still feel tempted to go further. We may want to try and understand why it is that particular neuroses have hit us in this time of crisis. We are now able to see that these were really a symptom of our illness. But we might still feel puzzled, disturbed even, as to why certain thought patterns have caused us such anguish. Where did they come from? CBT is good first aid, but it does not deal with these issues—it doesn't purport to—and so we might consider looking to more psychodynamic forms of counselling. These are the forms of therapy that have their roots in theories of psychoanalysis pioneered by Sigmund Freud, but continued by others, including Carl Jung (who certainly did not share Freud's atheistic views). In my own case, I found that God was able to shine his light on those areas of my mind where I was in such agony, and help me understand why these things had become so distressing to me. I am reminded of what one friend calls "the treasures of darkness", and the passage in Isaiah from which the phrase is taken:

> I will give you the treasures of darkness, riches stored in secret places, so that you may know that I am the Lord, the God of Israel, who summons you by name.[40]

Talking certain things through with others—friends as well as counsellors—has also helped me. A friend once told me that she would like nothing more than to sit on a therapist's couch and talk for hours, but I know that's not really me. I do know that many people benefit from joining support groups, and it is a slight regret of mine that I did not do this. I should have talked more. Perhaps, if I am honest, this book is a bit of a substitute for that.

The idea of "facing our fears" often features in popular culture, whether as the moral of a Disney film, or as something involving creepy crawlies and celebrities in the Australian jungle. But the type of fear we have to tackle in depression is of another dimension altogether. This is not only because depression itself is a terrifying experience, but also because, like a sniffer dog, the illness seeks out all our memories of what has caused us to be fearful in the past, finds them, and then intensifies them in ways unimaginable. We have already talked about how running away from what is causing us pain can make matters worse. To quote Gerard Hughes again, fear then becomes "a ruthless tyrant pervading and poisoning every aspect of our lives".[41] Although psychodynamic therapies may well help us come to terms with the fears involved in our suffering, a potential problem with them is that they can spend *too much time* focussing on negative experiences from our past, and this may be difficult for some people. We just need to be careful that dwelling on things that are too painful at this stage of our recovery does not set us back. If you are still battling with certain thoughts and emotions, and still wrestling with inner voices that seem determined to destroy your peace, you might want to consider the following advice (I have certainly found this helpful). The thing is, you say to the thoughts that are troubling you that you aren't going to play at wrestling any more. Instead, you take what Christian psychiatrist Glynn Harrison describes as a "reckless" approach to our negative thoughts. You dare to even enjoy rebutting them. This is not an unhealthy form of thought-suppression, but rather an attempt to reclaim the freedom God intends for us in our thought-lives. We just say firmly to our negative thoughts that we are not going to let them define us. "Insist on telling them that you don't care what they think about you, and you don't even care what you think about you."[42]

Don't forget; you are still unwell. And you are so much more than your thoughts.

6. SSSHH!

But I have stilled and quieted my soul;
like a weaned child with its mother, like a
weaned child is my soul within me.

Psalm 131

This business of learning to think differently requires space and patience. But space is probably not going to be a problem if you have suffered from a major depression and are having to take time off work to recover. In fact, this could well be one of the most space-filled times of your life. It is not going to be an enjoyable experience, but we can still seek to make the most of it.

I am going to suggest that you will also need silence. Buckets and buckets full of it. You may even want to throw in a couple of skip-loads for good measure.

If your experience of breaking down is anything like mine, there will be a lot of running round at first. Lots of phone calls and appointments—doctors, therapists, more doctors—all interspersed with trips to the pharmacy. Then, after the initial crisis subsides a little, the people around you will slowly (and quite rightly) go back to picking up their own routines, leaving you alone. In silence. I can't remember feeling too intimidated by this necessary form of abandonment, but I do remember feeling very grateful to have a companion on the journey into silence that was to follow. My companion took the form of Fr Christopher Jamison OSB, the presenter of a gentle yet captivating TV programme which happened to be screening during those initial weeks of my illness. *The Big Silence* featured five volunteers from various different backgrounds, all with fairly demanding jobs and domestic situations. They shared an openness to the idea of bringing some kind of new quality or depth to their lives—some more than others seemed open to the possibility of this experience having a religious dimension to it. Fr Christopher invited them to discover the transformative qualities of silence. This would involve entering into a profound silence, requiring not only the reduction of external noise, but also the quietening of heart and mind. This voyage inwards proved to be a pretty hard slog at times for the volunteers. In particular, fairly early on in the series, they struggled with the demands of a silent, eight-day residential retreat at a Jesuit Spirituality Centre. The retreat seemed to start fine, but it was not long before each of the volunteers hit some kind of emotional wall. The deepening silence had begun to expose all kinds of issues that had been suppressed by the daily grind and distractions of their lives, but which now seemed to vie for attention, causing complete confusion and turmoil within.

It is perhaps not surprising that we may feel threatened or uncomfortable with silence. Noise is all around us. Noise is the norm. I remember a question on a game show where the contestants had to come up with examples of places where people had to be silent. They really struggled, but eventually they came up with "church" as an answer. I'm not sure whether Christians of certain denominations or traditions would immediately associate their experience of church with silence and stillness! I once heard of a family who, uncomplainingly, had started wearing earplugs to their church in order to make the experience more bearable for them. As a fairly enthusiastic musician, I am likely to be one of the first to feel frustrated if someone complains that they found the drums too loud during the service (even if they were). I also appreciate that energetic services can be a sign of spiritual life in a church. But I think there can be an assumption sometimes that church is a place where we are meant to feel happy, and that happiness tends towards making a loud noise rather than being quiet and still. Aren't all the best parties noisy ones? If noise levels remain consistently high in our services, with the interspersed silences taking on a rather token role, our worship loses its texture. Not only are we probably poorer for trying to emulate the noisy world outside, but in the process, we have potentially alienated those whose mental state cannot cope with it. I think one of our mistakes when we approach this issue is that we assume children cannot cope with silence. Some anecdotal evidence of my own as to how children can respond positively to silence is based on watching my daughter's climbing lessons. One of the young teachers sometimes incorporates a period of silence half way through the lesson. It is as if the silence builds rhythm into their programme, creating space for some reflection on what they have just been doing and providing a much-needed rest before tackling the second half of the lesson. The silence almost engenders a sense of respect for the challenges of the bouldering wall. If silence can be built into climbing lessons in this way, why do we seem to shy away from silence when it comes to teaching spiritual truths to children?

It is a bit of a family joke that my father always likes to turn on music whichever room he is in, a trait which I think I have inherited. Before getting sick, part of my morning routine used to be switching on the radio as soon as I woke up. This was partly to get my first hit of the latest news but also, I think, to have some instant-morning-company. However, when my sleep patterns were completely ripped apart by the depression, and I often woke with strong feelings of anxiety, I no longer switched the radio on. The silence was more bearable. In fact, I dreaded the rest of the family getting up and having to listen to them perform their morning routines, without me.

Like me, you might find that your default option of using noise to fill the emptiness, or providing a distraction from things that you would rather not dwell on, has been sucked away by your depression. You might be more extrovert than me, and normally benefit from additional aural stimulation (introverted types often have a similarly healthy preference for silence). In your depressed state you might find that you cannot cope with anything but silence. But you will also hopefully discover the therapeutic effect of silence, and will even start to cultivate it, rather than merely tolerate it. As we learned in the previous chapter, our thoughts, emotions and behaviour are all interconnected—toxically so, in our depressed state. But by changing our *behaviour* (the "B" in CBT), with silence being the key ingredient in becoming more still and physically relaxed, we find that we can start to break the vicious triangle of thoughts-emotion-behaviour. Or rather, we start going round the triangle more slowly, and maybe even in a different direction than previously. We find that our thoughts become less anxious or invasive, and our mood may also improve.

Henri Nouwen once described our inner lives as being a bit like monkeys jumping up and down in a banana tree.[43] I would suggest that in the case of someone who is clinically depressed it is as if each of those monkeys has a jackhammer to boot. At first, silence seems only to amplify the noise. But as we settle into silence and build on the techniques we discussed in the last chapter, we find that we begin to distance ourselves from the monkeys in the tree; we stop putting our energy into trying to shut them up and snatching away their jackhammers. We just let them carry on doing their thing. And, gradually, they lose our attention. We learn to simply observe the thoughts that pop into our head, rather than judging them or engaging with them. We use diaphragmatic breathing as a focal point here—by coming back to our breathing, we not only centre ourselves, but we also find detachment from what is going on around us. And by attending to our bodies—from head to toe is a good way as any to do this—we learn how to relieve the tension, letting the various muscles relax.

There are various resources that can be used to help you learn these techniques in more detail.[44] I can appreciate the reluctance of people to look much further, though, because the worry is that it all sounds a bit like yoga. OK, I'm going to shock you, but I did actually buy a yoga book at one point. It even came with a DVD of a middle-aged leotard-clad female instructor demonstrating the various movements with considerable patience and kindness. There was no talk of any spiritual dimension to the exercises; I just found spending time concentrating on different parts of my body in a slow methodical way to be a soothing, grounding experience. It was if becoming aware of and focussing on my hands, limbs and feet was providing with me with some much-welcomed respite from the mental turmoil that I was living with 24/7. I don't think any of this undermined my Christian faith, and am not at all sure that we should feel inhibited about availing ourselves of what appear to be natural (and so presumably, God-given) ways of relieving tension and stress in mind and body. Indeed, there is probably much that we can learn here and apply to meditation that has a more specifically Christian focus.[45]

The volunteers on *The Big Silence* were all tempted to give up on silence, as was I sometimes. Silence can make certain aspects of our personality "kick off", and this can be extremely painful. I am reminded here of something the hostage Brian Keenan said about his experience of captivity: "I was forced to confront the man I thought I was and to discover that I was many people. I had to befriend these many people, discover their origins, introduce them to each other and find a communality between themselves and myself."[46] When our nervous systems are functioning normally, we tend to take it for granted that we have different sides to our personality, some complementary, some conflicting. But when we break down, these multiple "selves" each take on a new autonomy, and start pulling us in all sorts of different directions. It is likely that our fearful, impatient and judging selves clamour most. But where have the others gone—didn't we once have a hopeful self, a nurturing self, a creative self? And any notion of "the real me", our Who Centre, can seem a distant memory. I find Keenan's acceptance of his psychological discomfort and his attempts to bring about a kind of reconciliation within himself deeply impressive. He seems to have had an intuitive sense that only through being kind to himself was the work of self-reconciliation going to succeed. Although not writing from any conventional religious viewpoint, he seems to be demonstrating a spiritual awareness that our natural human inclination to blame ourselves for our predicaments can be dangerously life-draining and destructive.

Rowan Williams points out that the burden of taking up a positive form of "self-accusation", of being healthily suspicious about what our own hearts prompt and of relying instead on God to lead us into truth and honesty, is a *light* burden.[47] Didn't Jesus promise it to be thus? And yet, tragically, we choose to reject this light burden and instead take up much heavier burdens; burdens that sap our energy, such as endlessly justifying our actions to ourselves, or beating ourselves up about our various failings, or scoring ourselves against our neighbours, or, more tragically still, against fellow Christians. And at times of crisis, it seems that the temptation to do this becomes greater as we lash out in frustration and confusion. In those early days of illness, I became aware of a parting phrase used by some people towards me, particularly those who, it turned out later, had been acquainted with mental illness themselves in some shape or form. These kind people would tell me, rather earnestly but still lovingly, that I should "*look after*" myself. I do not think anybody had ever said this to me before, at least not with such meaning. I remember feeling challenged by these commands. They helped me become aware that in many ways I had probably not been looking after myself for some time, and that this had contributed towards the illness that had befallen me.

My feeling is that Christians struggle with the idea of self-compassion—why so? We might think there is not a great deal of room for self-compassion if the focus of our lives is about looking outwards in sacrificial service; didn't Jesus say we had to deny self? And the line between self-compassion and self-regard can feel like such a dangerous one to tread that we might feel it is safer to avoid being self-compassionate altogether. Perhaps it is not surprising, then, that any attempt to be "kind to ourselves" can be met with a degree of suspicion, even opposition, in the church. Julian Mann, writing in the *Church of England Newspaper*, aims his fire at the self-esteem movement, with what he describes as its "mantras" of "you're special", "learn to love yourself", and "believe in yourself".[48] And he has strong words for Christians who claim that we have to learn to love ourselves before we can love others: "A divine command intended to counter the fallen human tendency to self-love, selfishness and greed is shamelessly inverted." Ouch. It is, of course, right to point out the dangers of ego-boosting and ego-pandering. But we need to be careful not to throw the baby out with the bath water here. We are all damaged people, but words that criticise the concept of self-esteem will sound like a particularly loud clanging cymbal for those who struggle a great deal psychologically to come to terms with difficult and painful things that they have had to endure in their lives. Self-esteem can also be at uncontrollable rock bottom for sufferers of depression, who are in need of kindness *from themselves* like never before. There is even evidence to support the view that developing a compassionate mind-set towards ourselves could help the recovery from depression. "Compassion Focused Therapy" (CFT) recognises that we use various different "systems" to regulate our emotions.[49] These systems are often out of balance in people suffering from emotional distress. The "soothing system", which we normally draw on to provide a sense of relief and calming, can be particularly difficult to access. In CFT, one of the ways the therapist works with the client is to help them re-develop an internal compassionate relationship with themselves, to replace the blaming, condemning and self-critical one that has taken over.

I appreciate that CFT is only one therapy on a veritable smorgasbord of therapies, and that, often for good reasons, Christians will want to challenge the theories behind some of these. But being kind to yourself is something of a given in all of them, and I keep coming back to thinking that this should be a given for Christians, indeed especially for Christians. We are told that we should be a people clothed with compassion, kindness, humility, gentleness and patience, bearing with each other and forgiving whatever grievances we have against one another.[50] And it just isn't obvious to me why we should not be expected to show the same qualities in our dealings with ourselves, as with other people. As Glynn Harrison points out: "Rather than punishing ourselves harshly when we fail, or pitting ourselves against others, trying to prove we are better in endless games of comparison, we need to show ourselves the same kindness, patience and forbearance that God shows us."[51] And, interestingly, far from becoming self-absorbed or self-obsessed, when we develop an attitude of self-compassion we might start to feel the focus of our attention shifting away from ourselves. As Nick Thorpe puts it: "Oddly, self-compassion leads me ultimately back outwards towards others."[52] As the silence deepens further, we may also learn that finding communality between the different voices and personalities within us leads us towards discovering a new unity within ourselves, and a new unity between ourselves and God. In this process, I come to appreciate, maybe for the first time, that I really am one, unique, person, called to enter into a relationship with my loving creator, who is also One, within the relationship of the Trinity.

I hope you are still with me. Don't worry if some of the ideas discussed seem far from your current experience. I said at the start of this chapter that our dealings with silence will require space and patience before we begin to feel its therapeutic benefits. But at the same time, we should not feel burdened by any of this. We might do well to listen to this lovely piece of advice from Sebastian Moore OSB, gently admonishing anyone who falls into the trap of making their journey into silence and closer union with God feel like hard work:

> Now to hear what God is saying to us, we need
> to stop completely the mental noise. And this
> is easier than we think; all that I have to do is

realise that talking to myself makes two of me, me and myself, and this can't be true, so I can let this me-with-me collapse into just me, and that's where God is and has been all along. There are not two of me: love makes me one. It's a bit of a shock at first, but take a few breaths, and say, "OK, I'm here, God. Your move".[53]

Maybe it's time we re-joined the dance.

7. BACK TO LIFE

*The thief comes only to steal and kill and destroy; I have
come that they may have life, and have it to the full.*
John 10:10

The comedian Ruby Wax has devoted a lot of time
to learning to understand the illness which has often
afflicted her. Through her comedy she has put herself
out there, helping to raise the profile of depression and
bring understanding to both the initiated and ignorant
alike. She has described her approach to getting better
as a mixture of "honesty, humour, self-acceptance—and
medication".[54] And I can say Amen to that, irrespective
of whether Ruby's humour is always my cup of tea. In
many ways, it is a summary of what we have discussed in
this book so far. But what does this approach to getting
better look like in practice? As we start our climb back
up, we understandably want to know what changes we
might need to make to our day-to-day living; changes
that can promote and sustain our recovery.

It is important to remember that our recovery-lifestyles
are going to be different for each of us; they will reflect

our unique personalities and particular circumstances. I hesitate, therefore, before saying too much, for fear of sounding too prescriptive. And yet, just as I believe there is a common wisdom learned by those who have fallen over the edge and climbed back up, there can also be a shared application of this over-the-edge wisdom in the ways we approach our daily lives post-breakdown.

I have a friend who, if you ask him a question, often responds by saying "honest answer?" before going on to give his more considered response. It's so true that in a lot of our dealings with each other, we spend our time skating around issues, spinning things and indulging in platitudes. When my friend prefaces the answer he wants to deliver in this way, at least you know you're going to be getting the real deal. Ruby Wax advocates honesty in our dealings with depression. Being honest involves starting with where we are, and not where we would like to be. The likeable lead character Tim in Richard Curtis's feel-good film *About Time* devotes much energy to trying to change the previous events of his life—not always successfully, it has to be said—by using the secret time-travelling power that is endowed on every male member of his family. Earlier on in the film, Tim mainly uses his powers to improve his chances in his own romantic exploits. As the film develops he becomes more altruistic (in one scene he attempts to rescue his sister from an abusive relationship by manipulating events at the party where she first met her boyfriend). But the film ends with the voice of an older Tim explaining how he eventually stopped using his time travelling powers altogether, those same powers having taught him the importance of living in the moment, and making each day count.

There are similar lessons for us time-bound folk also. Jesus Christ is the same yesterday and forever, but he is also the same today, and that is where we experience him, even during the most fraught and painful days of depression; days that we might have spent writhing, quite literally, in pain, and which we desperately want to write off as not having existed at all. Instead of trying to erase time, let us try and use the present to discover where the healing is already taking place. As I have already said, you can be sure it is there, if we have eyes to see it. When we are faced with one of those nightmarish days, can we possibly summon up enough strength of mind to say to ourselves, and to God, that we are not going to write this day off, and to trust that out of the dreadfulness we are going to learn something which is only available as a result of our immediate circumstances? Remember: the facts are kind, so we may as well inhabit them rather than trying to run away from them. I think by doing this, or even by giving it our best shot, we could be tapping into something really powerful in the depression-disarmament process. We will also be fulfilling our vocation as Christians to live with fullness of life. Living with fullness of life is probably different to what some people would describe as "living life to the full". The latter is, I accept, not easily achievable when curled up in a ball under the duvet. But the former is always open to us, even when we are in the depths of our depression. Whatever type of suffering we go through in life, we need to try and grasp the truth that our life is not in some way on hold until we get better. God hasn't left us. Our sick bodies (and minds) are still temples of the Holy Spirit, and we can feel comforted, even liberated, by remembering that, in this sense, "we are not our own".[55]

Maybe it's just me, but I wonder if having been over the edge explains why it jars somehow when I hear people say, almost without thinking, that they are "good" when asked how they are. Firstly, what do they mean by "good"? The first definition for "good" in my dictionary is "having the right or desired qualities", and that might be why I detect a hint of smugness or self-satisfaction in this usage of this word. I can't also help thinking of Jesus when he said that only God is "good",[56] the idea being that human "goodness" is only relative to the goodness of God and is not to be found in our own resources.[57] I think the real frustration, though, comes from a sense that these people who claim that they are "good" must have some things on their mind that should be rocking their equilibrium, at least just a little bit. And if they don't, they are probably living a cocooned existence, which they may consider to be "good", but is unlikely to involve living with fullness of life. I have wondered what Jesus's answer would have been if someone had asked him during his ministry how he was doing. I can picture him remaining silent, at least for a while—in a contemplative way, but also slightly confused by the question. I once heard Sister Wendy Beckett saying something in an interview about not really believing in talk of being "happy" or "unhappy", the point being that life was simply about giving to God whatever we experience. Whilst we should feel free to enjoy the things of life when they are set before us—indeed I think Sister Wendy went on to say in the same interview that we have a duty to do so—we should never hold any expectation of "having a good time". So, don't believe the lie that the bad days don't count.

And when we are tempted to cast our depression as the thief who comes to steal and destroy our fullness of life, try to understand that it is not surprising, from a neurochemical perspective, that we are experiencing an inability to interact or concentrate or enjoy things. Our body is shutting down in this way because it thinks that is the best way to protect us and, ironically, to help us recover. The healing process is underway. So, remembering to be kind to ourselves, we must join in and help rehabilitate our shut-down bodies, dipping our toes in the waters of daily activity again. This is an incredibly difficult task. Do too much and we face confidence-busting blips. Do too little and we reinforce our body's inclination to retreat.

One thing which does not have to involve any significant social interaction when we are still in recovery mode is physical exercise. For me, running has been a good companion on the road to "normality". I suppose I was a moderately keen runner anyway, and I appreciate that, for some readers, putting on their trainers and pounding the streets is their worst nightmare. If running is not your thing, maybe cycling is, or speed walking, or hiking. If you are up to team sports or something involving another player, then that's great. But I deliberately highlight the more lonely pursuits as I see them almost as an extension of the silence that we discussed in the last chapter. This is solitude with legs; a solitude that can help us connect with the wider physical realm. Swimming probably works too. My philosophical French friend told me once that the reason he went swimming regularly was because he thought it was good to spend some time each week being in a "different medium", and maybe there is something in that. The thing is that whatever exercise we do, we improve not only our physical health but also our mental health. It's all about those neurotransmitters again, as well as reducing the levels of cortisol, the stress hormone. Nothing too ambitious at first; don't set unrealistic goals that may lead to disappointment if not met. But when we are able to hit targets that we set ourselves, we enjoy feeling a much-needed sense of achievement. The main benefits of regular physical exercise are probably experienced as a cumulative effect over a period time. Try also to discern when exercise is not what is needed. I know that sometimes a run can be just what I need to relax or unwind, but I have also made the mistake of forcing myself out running in a depressed state believing the exercise might work as a kind of antidote, when all my body really wanted was rest and a cup of tea.

And the good thing about these solitary physical pursuits is that you can take your trusty generic MP3 player with you (I haven't checked, but I imagine they probably do waterproof versions for the swimmers). As I have already said, for me music has been a great healer, so take your favourite moody music with you as you exercise. There are also some fantastic resources available to download—feed your soul whilst you run with Christian daily meditations, or listen to podcast sermons by your favourite preachers. By introducing human conversation through our earphones, we are further helping the rehabilitation process, the re-entry to daily living. But we also need to be careful that we don't end up crowding out these opportunities to be silent and mindful. This even seems to be good advice for those training to simply be better runners:

> And don't get caught up in trying to distract yourself by hiding between your earphones: Why blot out the real world? Be aware of your body and your feelings. Wherever you are, there will be something to be savoured. Enjoy the sounds and smells around you—the twitter of birdsong, the whisper of the wind, the salty tang of the sea, and the sweet aroma of the rhododendrons. Whenever you're running, your senses will be heightened. Allow your running to be

a pleasurable, sensation-filled experience. And
don't get overly tangled up in the technicalities
of training regarding heart rate monitors and
training zones.[58]

At some point we will feel ready to move on to social
company, but we might still hesitate. Looking back,
spending time in cafes was, for me, a useful stepping-
stone towards fuller engagement with the body public.
I enjoy a good cup of coffee and cafes have always stood
for comfort in my mind. As a kid, a trip to the shops
with my Mum would not be complete without visiting
one, where I would enjoy some long-anticipated hot
buttered toast. The beauty of cafe-life as a recovering
depressive is that it can be a relatively safe place to be, a
place where you can feel part of what is going on simply
by being there as a paying customer.[59] Spend enough
time in the same cafe and you get to know the staff, and
recognise the regulars, again without much need for
interaction. It is strange that even by connecting with
other people on this relatively passive level, you also
connect with yourself. I suppose it is to do with our being
made to relate to other people as well as to ourselves and
God. Certainly some of my best or most creative ideas
have come to me in cafes, and it is in cafes, especially
my favourite cafe, where writing has come to me most
naturally and freely. Meeting up with friends again can
be a real toughie. I think I probably took my lead from
the friends that stayed in touch—even if only by the

shortest of texts. I know the ones that don't contact you are only concerned that they are going to say the wrong thing, or that they will intrude in an unwelcome fashion. I also think that some people are frightened by mental illness and so they don't feel up to being confronted by it through a friend's suffering. Whatever their reason for keeping their distance, please don't be hard on them. But the ones who do stay in touch are probably signalling, consciously or sub-consciously, that they do feel up to it, if you feel ready to talk.

And when you meet up, their familiar company is such balm. Again, connecting with friends brings connection with yourself. By spending time with you, your friends are demonstrating their faith in you, and reminding you that you are still you, the person they know and like. It is not long before you can even share laughter together, healing laughter, the humour which Ruby Wax recommends. Let the humour become contagious, extending to laughing at yourself, at your situation. I have found the comic relief of a wry smile to myself in the worst of times seems to have a powerful sanitising effect on my situation. It's as if I'm doing a sideways glance to the camera (viewers of the TV programme *Miranda* will be familiar with the device) and saying, "OK, any ideas for how I'm going to get out of this?"

Don't feel guilty if you find spending time with friends easier than spending time with your family. Your family are going through the mill with you and don't have the same level of distance which your friends have for protection. Family members may not seem able to laugh about things, not yet. Oddly, I have found family get-togethers some of the worst things to cope with—I guess this is something to do with wanting my family, the ones who care for me the most, to know that I am getting better and am still my old-self, and that they really don't have to worry any more.[60] But often this has ended up heaping pressure on me, which has backfired in some quite spectacular ways.

Here we have hit on one of the biggest problems that we need to deal with if we are going to get properly better: the need to manage our own expectations of ourselves. Remember that we are dealing here with the Curse of the Strong, and for some their strength has been their reliability. "Want something doing? Then give it to me" might have been their motto. Until now. We have to realise that, at least for a while, we are no longer fully dependable. Saying no to people is a skill that we may never have really thought about developing. And, if we are really prepared to put things under the microscope, maybe part of our wanting to be dependable and reliable derives from questionable motives. How much of our dependability is actually an unhealthy form of self-reliance, wrapped up in our pride about how we like to be seen by others? If so, it could be time for a radical change. Is this another tough lesson, which only our experience of depression seems capable of teaching us? The effacement of our image as dependable and reliable will be incredibly painful. We might question whether, if we lose this, our ability to be a good parent, teacher, minister, or whatever might go with it. How will we pay the bills if we cannot function as our normal reliable self? But God is with you, even amidst all this catastrophising, and he will bring you out of your predicament by means you would never have been able to imagine. This could be one of the most liberating things you might ever do. It's time to let go.

It's also time to let go of trying to run your recovery. I used to tell myself that it would all be over in three months. After the three months passed, I said it would be six months. But still, it did not end. Then at some point I realised there was no point trying to work out that sort of stuff for myself any more. The thing is, the illness never ends really, not in any neat way such that we can demarcate our life pre- and post-recovery. As Mark Rice-Oxley puts it beautifully:

> Is that all there is? I ask, of myself, of the illness,
> of the world. And I know the answer.
> It isn't.
> It never is.
> But it no longer matters.[61]

So, recognising that our illness may remain with us in some shape or form for a long time, let's try and refrain from beating it up when the setbacks come. Why not even dare to befriend it, rather than see it as the enemy? I have to say that I have a bit of an issue with the idea of

treating depression (or any illness) as something external
to our experience, including any corresponding attempts
to personify the illness as an "other". I therefore find the
widespread adoption of Winston Churchill's description
of his depression as a "black dog" a bit suspect. Having
said that, I love Matthew Johnstone's self-illustrated
masterpiece *I Had a Black Dog*, and in particular the
picture in one of the cartoons of a black dog looking
utterly, utterly bemused as the owner-sufferer gives him
a massive hug. The dog certainly did not see that one
coming. The psalmist recalls that when he came through
the shadow of death he laid a table *in the presence of his
enemies*. Revd Bob Mayo notes that in Psalm 23, the
psalmist "did not run for cover", and he relates this to his
own experience of suffering epilepsy. Just as the psalmist
made fellowship with his enemies, Mayo claims that "in
the same spirit epilepsy has become my new best friend".[62]
This also reminds me of when a nurse kindly corrected
me when I said that I was trying to "work *around*" my
depression—she pointed out that I might do better to
"work *with*" it instead.

If we listen carefully, we might find that our newly
found four-legged friend is trying to tell us what level of
activity we should not try to exceed during our recovery.
Maybe this level has always been our maximum thresh-
old; maybe by constantly doing more than this, we were
always going to end up sick. We might worry about falling
into that trap, of wanting to "do everything", again, and
we will look at ways of staying well and promoting a

healthier lifestyle in the next chapter. But, also, trust your body. Are you feeling particularly tired or run down? Are there any physical signs that you've been doing too much? It sounds crazy, I know, but, when I have reached my max, my left foot starts tingling and feels numb—a bit like pins and needles. I was certainly not aware of this phenomenon until I became ill with depression. When I told my psychiatrist about this, he probably thought what you're thinking, and he certainly declined to offer me any medical explanation. I still like to think that my tingling left foot is a manifestation of some neurological phenomenon. But even if this is just a psychosomatic response, I still find that it pays for me to try and listen to what my left foot is saying.

8. SUSTAINABLE ME?

The Lord will fight for you; you need only to be still.
Exodus 14:14

The weeks, the months—however long it takes—will pass, and eventually you will reach a landmark on your climb back to recovery. From this vantage point you can see that you have climbed a long way, and that even though the top of the mountain is still out of view, the steepest part of the climb is behind you. You may now be back at work. You may have resumed many of your previous activities, including social ones. You may be attending church regularly again.

But you are still unreliable.

It's likely that the plotting of your recovery onto a graph would still show some fluctuations. Hopefully these will be levelling off over time. But even if the depression is largely in remission, there may still be days, or even weeks, when you experience blips. Sometimes these blips might be more autonomous in nature. But often they will be triggered by some form of exertion, or the cumulative effect of activity. "Stuff" just builds up, and your reaction when this happens will now be different, on account of having suffered from major depressive illness.

So, to avoid the build-ups and the blips, we need to be smart about the way we review our activities, and I am including the enjoyable ones here, because "good stress" can present just as much (or even more) of a challenge as working too hard. I talked in the previous chapter about our bodies developing warning mechanisms, but these do not remove the need for us to avoid too much stress developing in the first place. Once engrossed in some activity or other, it can be relatively easy for us to lose our sense of perspective about whether we are overdoing things. Often the difficulty is that we do not know what our parameters really are, not least because these are constantly changing as our recovery progresses. There was a period early on when I seemed to find it particularly hard to get things right. I ended up buying a watch with an hourly chime, which I used as a prompt to take a few seconds out to consciously check how busy I was, each hour of the day. I no longer have to micro-manage my activity levels, but I still have to monitor them. For example, I now sometimes look back at the last forty-eight hours, checking for activity-spikes or any prolonged periods of exertion. I then see if there is any flexibility in my diary over the next forty-eight hours so that I can build in any recovery time that I think may be required. If there isn't any slack (but usually there is, once I think a bit more creatively), I say to myself that I should at least be cautious about taking on anything extra. Another thing I do is to reflect first thing on what the "reliable me" would like to achieve during the day in question, and then proceed by purposefully removing one or two things from the to-do list. This appeals to my rebellious streak!

At some point, you might find yourself challenged to take your time management to a more radical level. Listen to what Mike Riddell has to say:

> I find it necessary about once every three months to review my various commitments. They accumulate over time, like the accretion of barnacles on the bottom of a boat. Various employers of mine have found this intensely frustrating, as I am regularly seeking to vary the terms of my employment according to my circumstances in life, often in a downward direction. At one time I considered myself invulnerable—every next task was a challenge to prove myself capable of it. Too late I discovered that I had become hollow inside, and that I was losing touch with my children, for whom "quality time" became a euphemism for very little time. Only gradually did I find the courage to give up on some spheres of activity. Three things happened in consequence: nobody missed my contributions; I became better at the things that remained; and I began to remember what it meant to be a soulful human again.[63]

I am not proposing that we should all go and hand in our notice. Interestingly, this is something which David, one of the participants in *The Big Silence,* was tempted to do when he returned to work. He felt that the newly-found contemplative dimension to his life was incompatible with his hectic job managing a restaurant. Fr Christopher, during one of his post-retreat visits to the volunteers, wisely cautioned David against quitting, bearing in mind his particular circumstances and stage in life. But even if we might also be counselled against any major jettisoning of our commitments, I suspect that we can all probably engage in some form of de-cluttering that would not only promote and sustain our recovery from depression, but would also prove to be a worthwhile task in spiritual terms. When our lives are filled with too much stuff, we find it hard to relate to one another. We are more likely to become anxious or over-protective. Once de-cluttered, we become less risk averse and our horizons become less limited. It becomes easier to live lives that are more flexible and responsive. In his book *Less is More*, Brian Draper advocates living more "poetically", an idea that appeals to me. This might involve looking for ways to move "more slowly, deliberately, positively, without rushing or getting stressed".[64] I suspect that a lot of us can look back on our earlier lives as feeling more carefree, less prosaic. Perhaps we only tend to reconnect with this former "self" when we are away from work on holiday or caught up in the wonder of Christmas. Unsurprisingly, as soon as we're back at work we want to plan the next holiday. I think part of my recovery from depression has involved trying to recapture something of this freedom, this poetry, in my day-to-day living. I have found that this approach can bring a much-welcomed lightness to the toughest of days. It can even be fun to look for counter-cultural ways to punctuate the day with stillness; taking three or four minutes out of the busyness to take part in a short on-line meditation,[65] or to observe punctuation marks, such as waiting for the green light at pedestrian crossings.

Hopefully, by experimenting with these time-management principles and trying to simplify our lifestyles, we will reduce the frequency of those build-ups of activity, and in turn reduce the risk of blips. Whilst some blips are caused by exertion of some sort or another, others can be an anticipatory response to some event which we perceive as likely to be stressful. I have found that, in either case, sleep disruption has tended to herald the onset of the blip. We have already learned that sleeplessness is a neurochemical feature of the illness, and the reality for many is that this particularly unforgiving symptom persists well into their recovery, and indeed may never be fully left behind. I have already talked about how difficult I found the whole sleep thing. I don't think it helped that I have always loved my sleep. My parents often tell me that I was the sort of kid who would sleep anywhere, any time: "You used to be able to sleep on a washing line if you wanted to." You get the picture. Even now, with something resembling a normal sleep function eventually restored, I certainly no longer take a night's sleep for granted; I don't think I ever will. If you are trying to cope with resuming your activities and still facing difficulties with sleep, I think it is important to try and resist the urge to be dependable. Heaven knows it is easier said than done, especially when in a befuddled state during the early hours, but still, just try to hand the coming day over to God and say that you are prepared to take his lead as to what changes you should make to your schedule. We sometimes think that God isn't interested in the minutiae of our daily activities, but my experience is that he will guide you even in the small things, if you would let him. I remember that, by consciously entering into this trustful frame of mind, I would find that the dynamic of the blip would somehow change; there would be a much-welcomed release of anxiety, as I received a kind of assurance that the next day could take care of itself, somehow.

I talked in the last chapter about how we might want to go easy on our illness. One of the ongoing challenges during recovery is how to handle the frustration we feel at the way our nervous system still can't cope with certain situations or pressure points. This frustration isn't all negative; it is in part a testament to how much of a fighter you are. I once stumbled across an episode of *Desert Island Discs* where the guest was the architect Charles Jencks. As the interview developed, I learned that Charles's late wife Maggie had died of cancer, and that it was her experience of suffering from that illness which had led to the founding of the network of support centres known as "Maggie's Centres". I was intrigued by much of what Charles Jencks said, but what struck me most was his comment that he thought fighting was "a very bad metaphor" to use when talking about cancer. "The best attitude toward it is both to care a great deal and to not care at all—those people who can go in and out of both feelings often do the best."[66] Despite the major differences between cancer and depression, this comment resonated with me when I heard it, and it still resonates with me now. Yes, we need to be attentive towards our illness and its symptoms, and we must work hard at our recovery, but we cannot let what energy we have be consumed by the process. Sometimes we might do better to simply observe our recovery, almost dispassionately, and watch it unfurl in all its unpredictable wonkiness.

We can feel frightened, as well as frustrated. Frightened that the residual symptoms we are suffering from might lead to a full-blown recurrence of the illness. If you are still on medication, remember that this can continue to play a key role—both curative and preventative—even after you are feeling a good deal better. As a rule of thumb, the more serious the episode of depression, the longer you can expect to remain on the medication, even once the depression is mainly in remission. I know taking the meds is no fun, but it really is a small price to pay. I certainly came to see the medication as an invaluable safety harness, to protect me from slipping too far back down the mountain, if I ever lost my grip or foothold. It is also important to remember that everything you have learned so far is still with you. Surely we are never going to forget these insights that we have gained through our own gritty, hard-won experience. We are not talking about the sort of facts that you cram into your head for sitting an examination, but which within a couple of months have evaporated from your memory bank. Yes, we will need to shake the dust off some of the things we have learned from time to time; we may also need to occasionally re-enter a deeper silence to re-acquaint ourselves with the wisdom from over the edge. But ultimately, and to borrow from the imagery of 2 Corinthians 3:3, these things are not just written in ink in our journals (if we are keeping one) but are also engraved on our hearts.

We will also feel impatient at times, and will want to know how long our indisposition will last. Again, perfectly natural. But remember how we saw in the last chapter that the laying down of our right to be dependable and busy could be an important step in our recovery—I just wonder if we really want to be rushing to fully assert that right again. I know we shouldn't try and cling to our illness, but we may end up losing something special if we only see the ultimate goal of recovery as becoming a fully-functioning human being again. I know from my own experience that certain "achievements" I have made on the road to recovery seem to have come with corresponding spiritual setbacks, or lapses. It is as if, with taking one step of feeling better, I have sometimes moved a step backwards from feeling close to God (if I am totally honest, this has led to feelings of hypocrisy when writing certain sections of this book). Archbishop Oscar Romero famously said we should "aspire not to have more but to be more". Perhaps part of "being more" means that we should no longer aspire to *do more*. But be aware; this attitude is truly revolutionary. After all, we once were also conditioned to believe in the "good" of being busy. I would even suggest that to challenge such assumptions can bring us into tension with the culture of some of our churches. It seems even those in church leadership roles are not immune. Stephen Cherry has given a name to one illustration of how the busyness culture has infected church life; "Diaryopoly" is the game which he has seen "clergy unthinkingly, but competitively, play when trying to fix a meeting date and they all tell each other what is in their diaries when various dates are suggested."[67] Ouch!

I know Jesus devoted a lot of time to teaching about the dangerous consequences of sitting on our hands when attempting to live out the Christian life. Let's face it, Jesus did an incredible amount during his own ministry. Was I wrong, therefore, to have second thoughts when I read a comment in one church's notice sheet giving the congregation the heads-up that the following weekend was going to be "wonderfully busy"? I'm sure that the events planned were indeed going to be wonderful, but it just made me think whether we are sometimes trying to be busy for busyness' sake in our churches. As we tidy up after the last church event and start planning the next, it can be easy to fall into the trap of setting our own agenda somehow, and domesticating God in the process. Do we ever think about taking time out to try and discern what it might mean to *be more*, and to be open to the fact that being more might involve taking one thing off the schedule? Part of the problem can be that we think we are just too busy to pray, especially if we are carrying around an assumption that prayer is a bit of a slog even at the best of times. Or we might view our prayer time as an extension of our own to-do list; more agenda-setting. We assume prayer is all down to us, just like every other aspect of our lives. But as Bishop Michael Marshall observes, "In a real sense, we do not begin or end prayer, properly understood. God for his part is always working in us and with us to perfect what he has already begun." Now, if there is really something in that, if prayer really shouldn't feel like hard work and is a process that God has already begun for us and in us, then our whole perspective should change, radically. Bishop Michael again:

> So we take up our part in God's prayer for us and from our side, as we turn to the Lord and consciously rest in him, consenting and responding to the Holy Spirit who is poured into our hearts whenever we open up to him.[68]

This theme of resting, of being more passive in all aspects of our lives, has run throughout this book. Even when we are facing the most challenging of climbs during our recovery, there seems to be a call, if only we would recognise it, to stop striving, to be more aware, and to spend time in the moment. And so, as our recovery progresses and the temptation to become more active increases, we need to develop practices that help restrain us from being consumed by busyness again.

My therapist once pointed out to me that people with my personality type needed quite a bit of "time out" to reflect on and process things. This came as quite a revelation to me. If you are a fan of *The West Wing*, you may remember that one of President Bartlett's favourite phrases was "What's next?" Bartlett tended to shout this out as he marched down the corridors of power with his army of advisers and assistants following in his wake. He seemed to thrive on resolving national and international crises, picking them off, one after another. But he was a complex character (brilliantly played by Martin Sheen), and could also be found in reflective mood, staring out of the window of Air Force One, his mind preoccupied no doubt by the myriad issues he was having to deal with. As Jennifer Kavanagh points out, "no life is either completely active or completely contemplative. We all stand on a spectrum between contemplation and outward engagement, the balance renegotiated by each of us at different times of our lives."[69] Illness can so often be the game-changer in this negotiation, forcing us to re-examine where we stand on the spectrum. Even a self-confessed workaholic like Andrew Marr, who claims not to be a reflective or "deep" person, can still say that his experience of suffering from a stroke has meant that he definitely now sees the world differently: "You move more slowly. You suck up experiences more intensely and you live the day more."[70]

I have wondered why my therapist's advice took me by surprise. Perhaps part of me had wanted to emulate President Bartlett's "What's next?" attitude. But by concentrating on doing more rather than on being more, I think I had allowed my equilibrium to get knocked, for too long. By not giving myself permission to have more down-time, more time to think, or play the piano, or just kick the leaves, I had, quite literally, been hurting myself. Later on, and in similar vein, my psychologist recommended that I should devote some time each evening to review the day, as part of a mental winding down process aimed at promoting a restful state of mind in preparation for bedtime. As it happened, I had actually already started doing what my psychologist was advising me to do (to a degree).

You see, I had been so impressed by the Ignatian spiritual directors who had mentored the retreatants on *The Big Silence* that I had started doing a bit of my own reading about Ignatian spirituality (well, I had plenty of time on my hands). As someone brought up in the evangelical tradition of the Church of England, I confess to feeling a little sceptical about what I might learn from the Jesuits (the order which St Ignatius founded), whom I rather associated with militant religious zeal, often aimed against the spread of Protestant reform. I told myself, however, that the Jesuits were probably just like most other Christian movements in having a fairly complex history, and that I should at least approach the teachings of their founder with an open mind. All I can say is that when I dipped into modern Ignatian writers such as Margaret Silf and Gerard Hughes, I discovered a spirituality that seemed to reach parts of my mind and soul that no spiritual writing had previously done. The St Ignatius these writers talked about seemed to be someone who was mainly concerned with finding God in all things, particularly in the emotional realm. Ignatius believed that by discerning our emotions, we can also discern God's will. If our lives are directed towards God, then we should find that any feelings of creativity, of being satisfied and contented, are pointing us towards how our deepest, God-centred desires can be fulfilled. Conversely, when we feel negative or irritable, this can be a sign of how those desires are being frustrated, or where we are pursuing desires that are not God-centred.

And so it was that I had come across the practice of Examen, the prayer which St Ignatius thought people should pray once a day, even if it was the only prayer they prayed. During Examen, the pray-er plays back the day and reviews what things have enlivened him or her, and what things have had the opposite effect, saying sorry to God for not responding to him in the events of the day and asking for his guidance for tomorrow. Given the way depressive illness seriously distorts the way we feel, we probably have to be more mindful than others when reviewing our emotions in this way. That said, my own experience in this area has been one of mostly being able to discern the difference between my "normal" changes in mood, and those which have been altered or exacerbated by the depression, thus enabling spiritual practices such as Examen to remain beneficial.

I know that in our depressed state a sense of desperation can develop within us as we search for sources of support and comfort. The temptation to succumb to a more consumerist approach to spirituality—picking and mixing different things as part of an ultimate quest to find something that "works"—is probably stronger in us as a result. But, equally, our predicament may present us with a positive opportunity to encounter God in a new way. Based on my own experience, I would certainly encourage other sufferers to explore how different styles of prayer may prove to be beneficial to them at this uniquely sensitive and difficult time in their lives.

It's a difficult balance, and I suppose the key, as always, is to leave things to God.

EPILOGUE

I'm drawing to a close, and so it will soon be time to go our separate ways. I wonder how you view your recovery so far. Even if your ascent still feels as though it is in the early stages, I hope that you're experiencing some glimpses of new life and new light as you walk. It may be you don't feel you have enough perspective yet to appreciate what you have learned, and how you have already changed. But that will come.

As for me? How do I view this wretched, pain-stricken experience, this Big One that I suspected might come at some point but hoped it never would, this tumultuous fall over the Edge that at times seemed hell-bent on obliterating me? Somewhat incredibly, I do look upon it (mostly) as a life-affirming experience. It has certainly produced a new depth to my faith and, in totally unim-agined ways, has left me feeling much more like "Me". I have undergone a fairly revolutionary re-ordering of my priorities, and have somehow acquired an ability to create more meaning and space amidst the busyness and stress that can so often threaten to destroy. I think I have become less fearful of things and have developed a lighter way towards living—I have become better at letting go, better at living with uncertainty. And I am continuing to learn more of these things. Not so much when I am feeling "fine" (or "good") it has to be said, but more so during those times when I realise and come to accept that aspects of my illness still haven't left me, not completely.

I have also witnessed a strange kind of renaissance in various aspects of my life, and again my illness proves to be the real well-spring for this, even though at times it felt more like the antithesis. I have read books that I don't think I would have ever read. I have jogged for miles listening to new, downloadable sources of sustenance. I have cried and laughed through films that I would not previously have made the time to see, and have been left soaring by music heard at concerts that I wouldn't have thought were worth paying tickets for. I have visited all sorts of new places—home and abroad—and in them have found places of sanctuary and inspiration. And, everywhere, the warmth of human company. I have even written a book that I wasn't expecting to write.

And in all these things, it has seemed as if the God of Connections has been guiding me through the most unusual pilgrimage I could have ever dreamt of.

Would I have still preferred not to have gone through it all?

Honest answer?

I don't know.

NOTES

PREFACE

1. Reading people's own accounts of their illness can often make difficult reading, but I found *Underneath the Lemon Tree*, Mark Rice-Oxley's memoir of his breakdown, to be a very endearing companion, as well as refreshingly accurate in terms of describing what I was personally experiencing. Mark Rice-Oxley, *Underneath the Lemon Tree: A memoir of depression and recovery* (Little, Brown, 2012).

2. Norman Anderson, *A Lawyer Among the Theologians* (Hodder & Stoughton, 1973), p. 9.

3. Robert Burton, *The Anatomy of Melancholy* (1621), Pt. 1, § IV, Memb. 1. "Melancholy" or "melancholia" are terms that were previously used for depression.

4. See F32, "Depressive Episode", *International Classification of Diseases and Related Health Problems*, tenth revision: <http://apps.who.int/classifications/icd10/browse/2010/en#F32>.

1. WHY BOTHER?

5.   Margaret Silf, *Landmarks* (Darton, Longman & Todd, 1998), pp. 223–4.

2. THE BIG ONE

6.   Peter Meadows, *Pressure Points* (revised second edition; Kingsway Publications, 1993), p. 60.

7.   If you feel up to it, you might want to try listening to something like "Short Ride in a Fast Machine" by American composer John Adams. White-knuckle moodiness! In contrast, "The River Cam" by Eric Whitacre (another American composer) is probably one of the most wistful of pieces written for cello—highly recommended.

8.   Henri J. M. Nouwen, *The Inner Voice of Love: A journey through anguish to freedom* (Random House, 1999), pp. 116–18. Quoted by permission of Random House Inc.

9.   "Afterword", in Rachel Kelly, *Black Rainbow* (Yellow Kite, 2014).

10.   Quoted by Fred Vermorel, *The Secret History of Kate Bush* (Omnibus Press, 1983), p. 81.

11.   Dr Tim Cantopher, *Depressive Illness: The curse of the strong* (second edition; SPCK, 2006), p. 6. Quoted by permission of SPCK.

12.   Andrew Rawnsley, "Ten months remain for Ed Miliband to pass the blink test", *The Observer*, 22 June 2014. Quoted by permission of Guardian News & Media Limited.

13.   <http://www.telegraph.co.uk/news/politics/9332575/MPs-reveal-their-battles-with-depression.html>.

14. Luke 22:44

15. <http://www.dailymail.co.uk/news/article-2294686/Archbishop-Can-terbury-Justin-Welby-reveals-fears-following-father-alcoholism.html>.

16. Luke 14:28

3. HELP

17. Luke 17:33 (NRSV).

18. Quoted courtesy of Universal Studios Licensing LLC.

19. Gerard Hughes, *God of Surprises* (new edition; Darton, Longman & Todd, 1996), p. 158.

20. Rowan Williams, *Silence and Honeycakes* (Lion Hudson, 2003), p. 89.

21. Hughes, *God of Surprises*, p. 101.

22. Hughes, *God of Surprises*, p. 151.

23. Quoted courtesy of Miramax.

24. Alastair Campbell, "Response to Stephen Fry suicide interview shows attitudes are slowly changing", <http://www.alastaircampbell.org/blog/2013/06/10/response-to-stephen-fry-suicide-interview-shows-attitudes-are-slowly-changing/>.

4. MY BRAIN HURTS

25. A term used in Dr Joel Robertson with Tom Monte, *Natural Prozac* (HarperCollins, 1997).

26. See Preface, note 4.

27. Interestingly, Cantopher states that the only form of depression that he is writing about is "stress-induced depressive illness"; see *Depressive Illness*, p. xiiii. I subsequently found out that reading the book had proved to be a turning point for Mark Rice-Oxley, as he explains in *Underneath the Lemon Tree* (see Preface, note 1).

28. Cantopher, *Depressive Illness*, p. 52 (my emphasis).

29. Robertson with Monte, *Natural Prozac*, p. 32.

5. THINKING DIFFERENTLY

30. John White, *The Shattered Mirror* (Inter-Varsity Press, 1987), p. 32.

31. John Main, *Twelve Talks for Meditators* (Audio CD; 2012). Quoted by permission of by The World Community for Christian Meditation.

32. Silf, *Landmarks*, p. 31 et seq.

33. John Kirwan, *All Blacks Don't Cry* (Penguin Books, 2010), p. 58.

34. 1 John 4:18

35. Isaiah 43:3

36. Interested readers could consult Mark Willams and Denny Penman, *Mindfulness: A practical guide to finding peace in a frantic world* (Piatkus Books, 2011).

37. *Church of England Newspaper*, 21 March 2014.

38. John 3:8

39. Stephen Cherry, *Barefoot Disciple* (Bloomsbury, 2011), p. 115. Quoted by permission of Bloomsbury Publishing Plc.

40. Isaiah 45:3

41. Hughes, *God of Surprises*, p. 101.

42. Glynn Harrison, *The Big Ego Trip* (Inter-Varsity Press, 2013), p. 196.

6. SSSHH!

43. In fact, Nouwen has used this description several times; see, for example, "Moving from Solitude to Community to Ministry" at <http://www.rebuildjournal.org/articles/solitude.html>.

44. One of my favourites is the beautifully illustrated and very easy to digest *Quiet the Mind*, by Australian Matthew Johnstone (2011, Constable & Robinson Limited).

45. For a contemporary approach towards Christian meditation, I would certainly recommend investigating the various resources on offer from The World Community for Christian Meditation, <http://www.wccm.org>.

46. From Brian Keenan, *An Evil Cradling* (Hutchinson, 1991). Reproduced by permission of The Random House Group Ltd.

47. Williams, *Silence and Honeycakes*, p. 49.

48. Julian Mann, "Our obsession with self-esteem is damaging the church", *Church of England Newspaper*, 28 March 2013.

49. The psychologist Professor Paul Gilbert is closely associated with CFT. His book *Overcoming Depression* is on the NHS prescribed reading list—I listened frequently to this in audio format on my MP3 player, mainly whilst out running, and found it very helpful.

50. Colossians 3

51. Harrison, *The Big Ego Trip*, p. 166.

52. *Third Way*, April 2013.

53. Sebastian Moore, *The Contagion of Jesus* (Darton, Longman & Todd, 2007), p. 172.

7. BACK TO LIFE

54. Stephanie Merritt, reviewing Ruby Wax's show "Losing It", *The Observer*, 27 February 2011. Copyright Guardian News & Media Limited.

55. 1 Corinthians 6:19

56. Luke 18:19

57. See R. T. France, *Matthew* (Inter-Varsity Press, 1985), p. 285.

58. Julian Goater and Don Melvin, *The Art of Running Faster* (Human Kinetics, 2012), p. 31.

59. I appreciate that, for some readers, issues such as shyness, or concerns about feeling vulnerable in certain situations, might mean that different ways of starting the re-entry into public life might need to be explored.

60. I feel I ought to acknowledge here that not all of us are fortunate enough to have supportive, close families. Indeed, the lack (for whatever reason) of these relationships may be for some a contributing factor to the onset of depressive illness.

61. Rice-Oxley, *Underneath the Lemon Tree*, p. 301.

62. Bob Mayo, *Church of England Newspaper*, 28 August 2011.

8. SUSTAINABLE ME?

63. Mike Riddell, *Sacred Journey* (Lion Publishing, 2000), p. 54.

64. Brian Draper, *Less is More* (Lion Hudson, 2012), pp. 114–5.

65. I would recommend <http://www.sacredspace.ie> and <http://www.loyolapress.com/3-minute-retreats-daily-online-prayer.htm> for example.

66. *Desert Island Discs*, BBC Radio 4, 1 July 2012.

67. Stephen Cherry, *Beyond Busyness: Time Wisdom for Ministry* (Sacristy Press, 2012), note 10.

68. Michael Marshall, *The Transforming Power of Prayer: From illusion to reality* (Continuum, 2010), p. 118.

69. Jennifer Kavanagh, "Practical Mystics", *Third Way*, May 2013.

70. *Radio Times*, 21–27 September 2013.